NOTES TO MY CHILDREN

Frank Roseman

ATHENA PRESS
LONDON

ISBN 1 84401 321 9

First Published 2004 by
ATHENA PRESS
Queen's House, 2 Holly Road
Twickenham TW1 4EG
United Kingdom

Printed for Athena Press

NOTES TO MY CHILDREN

Introduction

Dear Children,

This notebook is my attempt to give you an easy-to-use guide on issues and questions which have concerned me in my life and which, I believe, had I possessed these views early on, would have made my life much more virtuous, successful and satisfying. I sincerely hope they are of some use to you.

Guidelines

How to achieve

- Happiness
- Success
- Wealth
- Peace of mind
- Correct eating
- Measurement
- Balance
- Power & Responsibility and Cost/Benefit

Questions answered

What drives everyone?

What is the nature of Life?

What to look for in a partner.

What should you aim for in life – and why?

What should you teach your children – and why?

Why do bad things happen to good people (and why do good things happen to bad people)?

Is there a God and if there is what is he like?

Praying – should you do it and does it work?

Can You Trust Them and How to Use Them

Accountants
Lawyers
The Government

Happiness

A young monk went to see his Abbot, 'Father, I find that I cannot live with my vow of celibacy and I must leave the Order.' The Abbot replied, 'My son, we understand this problem, it has happened to many novices before you and we have an answer for it. We have a barrel, located in yonder wood with an appropriately positioned aperture. Feel free to use it whenever the urge becomes irresistible.' The young monk was overjoyed and ran off to avail himself of the Monastery Barrel. He found the barrel of great benefit and availed himself of it on a regular basis until, one day, as he was walking towards it he met another young monk coming from the barrel. 'Where are you going?' enquired the returning monk. 'Why I'm going to use the Barrel,' said the young monk. 'No you're not,' replied the returning monk. 'Why ever not?' asked the puzzled young monk. 'Because it's your turn in it!' came the reply.

Summary
While our society is obsessed with happiness, very few people believe they know what happiness is. Happiness is a much abused word and concept – many people spend most of their life haphazardly searching for 'happiness', often confusing it with short-term pleasure; social recognition from family, friends, or society at large; or the sense of happiness that comes with the accumulation of material wealth. While all of these aspects of life can be part of happiness, they themselves, are not happiness.

Let's start off on our search for happiness with an attitude. (You don't have to, but it makes it easier) Assume the attitude that, 'I'm always happy – unless I have a reason not to be. In which case I fix the problem – or call Dad and he'll fix the problem – and then I can return to being happy again.'

I have a mantra that I recite to myself five times a day, every day, which I recommend to you should you ever feel unhappy. It is as follows:

Every day in every way I am happy unless I feel unhappy, in which case, I identify my problem then identify the answer, put the answer into practice and return to being happy.

It works.

What Happiness Is Not

As I said earlier, happiness is often confused with temporary euphoria – the sort of feeling that can be induced by casual sex, drugs, alcohol, a feeling of pleasure at someone else's misfortune or, even, exercise! While these activities can deliver a short-term feeling of pleasure they are not 'happiness'. Happiness is invariable associated with achievement and success through positive activity, and while physical exercise can deliver a short-term 'high', exercise in itself, unless part of a programme of physical aims, will not bring 'happiness'. Although regular physical exercise is, in my opinion, an essential part of a happy life.

Happiness, by its nature, has a relative definition and although it is highly relative to each person, most people will end up with the same answer in physical terms. So what is happiness?

True happiness is the feeling we experience when we feel we are succeeding in life.

To know that we have succeeded at something we have to establish a measure of what we have achieved. Writing down goals gives us that measure – we often forget how much we achieve in life. However, by writing down our goals, when they are important to us, when we do achieve them we have the pleasure of knowing that we have succeeded.

Happiness is the achievement of your written-down sensible goals.

Sounds simple? It is, it's very easy to do and it only takes a small amount of time and effort.

Life is a journey and like all journeys if you don't know where you are going you can't get there. The most important thing to know before starting out on any journey is where you are aiming to arrive. Know your destination. If it's a long journey you may also need to know your stops along the way – your subsidiary destinations – the steps you need to achieve to get to where you want to be.

Achieving happiness is also a journey, and to achieve it – to arrive at the destination of happiness – is relatively easy if you start out knowing what and where happiness is.

Only you know what would make you happy. You can, of course, if you don't like yourself, set impossible to achieve objectives that you decide would make you happy. You can choose to give yourself aims that are irrelevant to your life or will make no real difference to your physical, philosophical, or intellectual state. Aims, that when you achieve them, do not change your life or make you *happy*. You can choose to deceive yourself; that's your choice. However to achieve true happiness use the following system:

- Think of what you ideally believe would give you happiness and write it down. Make a list that covers all aspects of your life: health, work, income, friends, children, education, career, hobbies, holidays. Look to find corresponding or overlapping areas and integrate them where possible.

- Think about what you have written then write down what you believe are sensible relevant aims that, with thought and effort, you can achieve. Listing, if necessary, all the relevant subsidiary aims necessary to achieve your main goals.

- Give yourself a sensible time target for each goal or set of goals.

- Review what you have written and satisfy yourself that it is a comprehensive list of your wants and needs – if it is not – repeat the process until it is.

- Work out what you need to do in each area of your life to succeed in your aims and eliminate any contradictions. (For example, don't aim to party all night and study all day. Or, more realistically, if you want to lose weight plan to eat less, eat right and exercise more. If you want to become professionally qualified plan time to do your studies, in a manner that will mean you study at a time you are fresh and able to concentrate, and not after a hard day's work. If you want love – do those things that brings love)

Once you have decided upon your goals and written them down, review them frequently (some, you need to review daily, others, weekly, monthly and at the least, quarterly), and if you feel that you wish to alter them then do so – after all, they are your aims!

As you achieve your aims you will probably have evolved new aims – great – more happiness! Write them down and repeat the process! After all, permanent happiness has to be a continuous process because life, with its challenges and opportunities, is itself continually changing.

It is important to first set your ideal goals and then review them in the light of what you reasonably believe you can achieve. We are not attempting to make you super slim or super rich; we are aiming to make you happy. You don't have to stop dreaming – dreams are a great motivator and can usually be achieved if you give yourself enough time and set sensible intermediate goals. By all means aim towards them and enjoy achieving them by setting yourself goal steps that you know you can achieve.

Don't only set yourself aims that take a long time to achieve. Happiness is best achieved by having goals that are short-term (daily) medium term (weekly and monthly) and long-term (one to five years) as well as a general aim in life. That way you can experience happiness every day by achieving your aims.

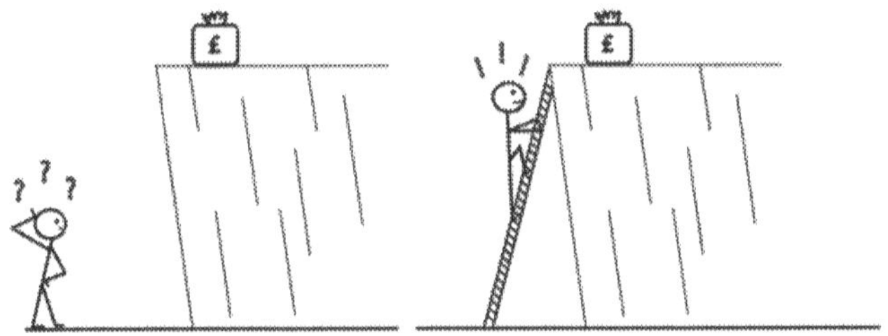

Attitude

Doctor:	Do you know there's a guaranteed remedy to the problem of apathy?
Patient:	Really, then why don't we see more people cured?
Doctor:	No one's very interested in taking it!

In my experience there are three factors that determine a person's success and happiness and they are: education, intelligence and attitude.

I have known and employed many very well-educated fools; people who had acquired large amounts of specialised information but could not employ it in a productive manner.

I have also known and employed many intelligent people, by this I mean people who, when motivated, could process information well, accurately and quickly. However, often they were uninterested in making efforts to benefit from their abilities.

Of the three factors the one I have found the most important in achieving success is attitude. Where a person has a positive and determined attitude, my experience has been that, he generally succeeds even if he (or she) had not benefited from a good education or was not exceptionally clever.

Of course an individual needs both a degree of natural intelligence, and a reasonable level of education, appropriate to the opportunity or challenge facing them. However, of these three factors a positive, determined attitude is by far the most important. With the correct attitude the necessary academic information can and will be acquired, and the ability to process the information (intelligence) will be developed.

Education and intelligence can be of great value, but without the correct attitude will achieve very little.

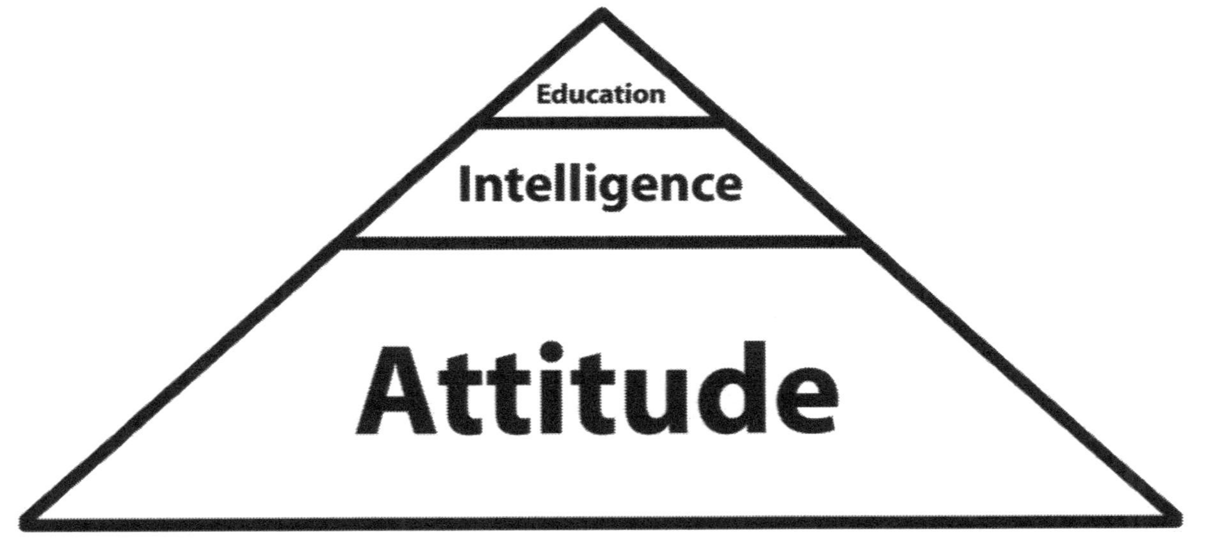

Attitude – the most important element in success

Needs and Wants

Summary
There are only two things in life you can never have too much of,
the first is understanding: a mixture of knowledge and wisdom,
and the second is wealth. With everything else, remember my
saying of, 'More than enough – is a burden'
In setting your happiness goals it's vital that you identify and
separate your needs from your wants. Needs are those things you
can't live without, while wants are those things that you can live
without but would enjoy having. Many areas are fuzzy, such as
food and career, both are a need and a want.

Think very carefully in identifying your needs, generally
speaking, they'll fall into three areas:

- philosophical well-being,
- physical well-being; and
- academic well-being.

Identify and give them priority and set aims which will improve
them. Always work to be aware of the difference between needs
and wants; never allow wants to trap you in situations that make
you unhappy.

It is almost certain that to achieve your needs you'll have to
sacrifice some wants, although you'll be pleasantly surprised how
often needs and wants coincide, and how by slightly adjusting the
timing or quantities of wants, both wants and needs can be
achieved. For example, I love chocolate but it makes me fat and
keeps me awake at night if I eat it late. So now I eat less and when
I do eat it I do so during the day – I haven't had to give up a want
– just be in tune with my body's needs.

So, in summary, to be happy all you have to do is:

1. Identify those achievements that would make you feel happy then write them down.

2. Identify the steps you have to take to achieve your listed goals and write them down.

3. Identify the obstacles you have to avoid or overcome, and again, write them down.

4. Identify the help you may require and write that down.

5. Plan your daily, weekly, monthly, quarterly, and annual activities, so as to allow you to carry out your programme.

6. Review your plan appropriately each day, week, month, or whenever you achieve an aim or experience a material problem.

7. Whenever you achieve one of your aims or sub-aims you should experience a sense of satisfaction or happiness. If you don't then review your aims to make sure that you have correctly identified what it is that you believe will make you feel happy and, if necessary, change your aims.

8. Always remember that, life is dynamic and that once you have acquired, or achieved, an aim your perspective will alter and you may decide that you have new aims that you believe will make you happy. That's okay and if you do decide to have new aims then simply repeat this process and enjoy life!

Happiness Plan

COMPLETE ONE OF THESE SIMPLE PLANS FOR EACH OF THESE THREE AREAS OF YOUR LIFE AND ANY OTHER AREAS OF LIFE YOU FEEL ARE APPROPRIATE FOR YOU. HEALTH, CAREER, BUSINESS, PERSONAL.

Main Goal

....

....

SUBSIDIARY GOALS
(STEPS I MUST ACHIEVE TO ACHIEVE MY MAIN GOAL)

1. ....

2. ....

3. ....

4. ....

5. ....
(ADD MORE STEPS IF YOU NEED THEM)

Obstacles I Must Avoid or Overcome to Achieve My Goals

1. ....

2. ....

3. ....

4. ....

5. ....
(ADD MORE STEPS IF YOU NEED THEM)

Help I Must Obtain to Achieve My Goals

1. ....

2. ....

3. ....

4. ....

5. ....
(ADD MORE STEPS IF YOU NEED THEM)

With your goals in mind, write out your daily, weekly, monthly, quarterly, and annual routines, each on a separate sheet of paper, for each of the three sections of your life.

Consolidate these sheets into one for each time period. (see example 1.)

Ensure that the time period routines harmonise with each other – daily with weekly, weekly with monthly, and so on.

Review what you have consolidated and ask yourself if what you are planning is sensible and reasonable. Confirm with yourself the belief that you can achieve it; if you can't, then review your aims and re-plan. When you have completed your programme then proceed to do it, starting from right now!

Follow your plan every day and review your whole plan once a month, at a time when you have the opportunity to carry out a relaxed review. If you feel that it can be improved on then do so.

Example I: My Daily Routines

07.00	Get up and run for one mile – or more, if I feel like it. Weight train and row.
08.00	Shower, have breakfast.
09.00	Check post, emails, and process correspondence.
12.00	Write.
14.00	Light lunch. After lunch meditate – siesta – for 10–20 minutes.
15.00	Write.
17.00	Tea, talk to my children. Review emails.
18.00	Monday, Wednesday and Friday visit gym with children.
20.00	Shower, then dinner.
21.00	If at home: TV, talk, games – boggle or scrabble – read.
24.00	Bed.

Success

A young man was marooned on a desert island along with a wild donkey and a large ferocious dog, which continually followed the donkey. After several months of enforced celibacy and no prospects of rescue the young man's thoughts turned to the donkey and he decided to engage the animal in a close personal relationship. Whenever, however, he attempted to become physically close to the donkey the dog would bark and attempt to bite him. Whenever he attempted to imprison the dog the donkey would attack him. This situation went on for several years until, one day, the young man noticed something struggling in the sea. He plunged into the waves and brought a beautiful young lady, scantily clad, to the beach. 'You saved my life,' she sighed. 'I'm so grateful, I'll do whatever you want, anything at all,' she said, giving him a languorous look. 'Marvellous,' he said, 'Just grab that stick and hit that dog while I screw that donkey!'

Summary
Success is that feeling we experience when we achieve an aim or a series of aims.

What is Success? – the Relative Definition

I believe that general success and happiness is the same thing. One has to achieve success to find happiness. It is impossible to be happy without also achieving some form of success. Of course, a narrow definition of success is possible where happiness is excluded, for example, passing an exam but losing a loved girl or boyfriend. This would mean that while one has achieved a measure of success one has not achieved overall happiness. It is therefore necessary in life to establish those things you believe are necessary to give you overall happiness. While happiness is the aim, success is the 'what' that must be done to achieve the aim of happiness.

How Does One Achieve Success in Life?

Define what it is you wish to achieve in your life and by when you wish to have achieved it.

- Write down your aims and your timescale.
- Write down the steps you need to accomplish to achieve your aims.
- Write down a plan to follow the steps you've identified.
- Follow your plan.

Review your plan frequently – if you find that you no longer want an aim don't be afraid to change or discard it. If your plan doesn't seem to be working then see if you can think of a better way to achieve your aim – if you can, then alter your plan – if you can't, then persist with your plan.

Success is the achievement of your written-down sensible goals.

I would, however, make the following observations:

> Success in life, as a whole, has to be defined as success in more than one area of life. It's necessary to define in all areas of your life, in which you wish to achieve success, what it is that *you* define as success. Health, career or occupation and domestic life, the old 'health, wealth and happiness' are the normal areas we look to succeed in, although they may each be broken down into several sub-sections and require separate goals.
>
> If you wish to achieve general success in your life you have to accept that you also want happiness too. I say this because I cannot envisage a state of happiness that is not also a state of success. The definition of success is within your control and therefore so is your happiness.

If you are looking to achieve success in only one area of your life then the following rules will make it possible.

1. Define what *you* see as success in your chosen area. Write it down with a timescale for its achievement.
2. Ask yourself if you really believe that your chosen goal is

achievable by anyone from your position in life and with your timescale. What you are checking here is that your aim is achievable, and that you are really committed to your own success by giving yourself an aim that can be achieved.

3. Work out short-term and medium-term aims that coincide with your main aim. Make sure that they are achievable by you in a lifestyle that you are able to live. Write them down with a timescale.

Put yourself into the habit of succeeding by setting easily achievable short-term goals that are compatible with your medium and long term aims.

4. Keep to your plan. If you can't, then decide if you want to change your aims, your plan, or your behaviour.

Deal with reality and not the illusions of society or political correctness. For help here see my notes on philosophy below.

5. Define your long, medium, and short-term aims, and ensure that they are consistent with each other.
6. Identify those groups, organisations, and individuals, who can assist you in achieving your aims. Plan how to use them if this is possible and desirable.
7. Identify those groups, organisations, and individuals, who can prevent you achieving your aims. Plan on how to avoid them if possible, or, if necessary, how to overcome them.
8. Identify those qualifications your aims require you to have to achieve them. Work out how you are to achieve these qualifications.
9. Identify any special qualities that you need to acquire to achieve your aims, then work to acquire those qualities.
10. Focus on achieving your aims. If you find that you cannot achieve them – review your aims to what you can actually do; you will probably find that you've only missed a step and your long-term aims are still achievable – you may only have to take a little longer or acquire an additional skill.

- Make a plan.
- Keep to your plan.
- Review your plan at regular intervals.
- Do not be afraid to change your plan if you see a better aim or your methods if you see a better way.

Sounds simple? It is.

Life is a journey and like all journeys if you don't know where you are going you can't get there. The most important thing to know before starting out on any journey is where you want to arrive; know your destination. If it's a long journey you may also need to know your stops along the way – your subsidiary destinations – the steps you need to achieve to arrive where you want to be.

What is Success – the Absolute Definition

The absolute definitions of success have to be from the minimums, as life, with its challenges and opportunities, can create situations where these are far below that which is available or desirable. I have established these minimums with my children in mind, although I am aware that in most cases they have been well exceeded.

Minimum success is achievement in three fundamental areas:

Philosophy: tells you where you are going and why you are going there.

Academia: shows you how to understand and how to arrive at where you want to be. To understand the sections of the world you live in and how to make them work for you.

Physically: ensures that you have the ability to complete your journey and achieve your aims and destination.

Philosophical minimums of success are:

- To understand the importance of children, a family, and a stable relationship.
- To understand that the real truth of life is in having children,

nurturing and educating them, so that they too are able to successfully realise the importance of having, nurturing and educating children.

- A family should consist of two parents and at least three children, with more if the parents want, and can afford, them.
- To understand that the State is not to be trusted and never relied upon. The State is the employment and career vehicle for millions of non-productive employees. Your interests are of no concern to the State, except as a mechanism of achieving the aims of the State's employees.

Academic minimums of success are:
- An average of 8 'Bs' at GCSE level, 3 'Bs' at 'A' level, a Second Class Degree in a Commercial or Scientific Course, and finally, to achieve a profession qualification that ensures you have the long-term security of a means of earning a living, doing what you are comfortable doing.
- To speak a second language so that, if required, you can relocate you and your family to a different country.

Physical minimums of success are:
- If you are a girl, then the ability to run a mile in under eight minutes and to be able to bench-press at least half of your own weight.
- A boy should be able to run a mile in under six minutes and be able to bench-press all of his own body weight.
- Your ability to use a martial art to successfully defend yourself, and your family, from a single aggressor.

Wealth

I've been unhappy when I was poor and unhappy when I was wealthy. But let me tell you, being unhappy when you are wealthy is much better! 'Money can't buy you happiness!' Whoever wrote that has never been wealthy; money can and often does buy you happiness!

The Three Rules of Wealth:
1. To spend wealth all you need to be is stupid.
2. To save wealth all you need to be is sensible.
3. To create wealth all you need to be is clever.

Summary

Why be wealthy? Be aware that although people are supposed to be 'free' and that we are supposed to live in a 'democracy', in fact most people are anything but free, and we certainly do not live in a democratic structure. In fact we live in a tolerant bureaucracy. However, the aware individual can become free by becoming wealthy – real freedom is economic freedom. Just about anything may be bought, anywhere in the world if you have the money.

The world is made up of four levels of people:

PRIVATE EMPLOYEES

Private sector employees are really State slaves that the State rents out. They pay most of the taxes and do most of the work. Their income is taxed before they receive it, and then further taxed when they choose to spend it, or even when they don't – as in T.V. licence fees, council tax etc. They have virtually no tax breaks. Furthermore they are subject to employment tax in that their employer's national insurance contributions are really a tax they have to pay through their earnings for their employer. (An employer has to calculate the full cost of employing someone when budgeting for his business and, of course, he cannot differentiate these costs, as they are a direct tax and therefore a cost of employment.)

THE SELF-EMPLOYED

Self-employed have a better deal than employees insofar as they can, if properly advised, reduce their tax burden quite materially (although the British Government is working hard to reduce their advantages). They also receive their income before tax and consequently have more choice and flexibility in how they account for their income.

BUSINESS OPERATORS

They have a much better deal and more freedom. They can run many of their expenses quite legitimately through their businesses. Unlike employees, and like the self-employed, they receive their income before tax, although they do suffer other taxes that they have to pay whether they are successful or not. For example, they have to pay a 'rent' to the Government for using employees, by way of national insurance contributions, and P.A.Y.E. tax, which is nominally deducted from their employees but which the employer has to fund. There are also numerous fees and licences as well as many regulatory penalties that can be arbitrarily inflicted by bureaucrats upon the business person. However, where there is a fundamentally sound business situation, with an interesting income stream, the use of limited liability companies is of great benefit. On a practical note, I always recommend that unless there is a strong reason to continue a company that it should always be closed down after one year (or less) and a new company introduced into the business activity. This crystallises most of the exposure to Government and limits their depredations upon the operators of the business. This does not normally need to have any real effect upon the business as assets – including name, goodwill etc. – can be sold to the new trading entity. The business operator should, ideally, use different directors and shareholders for each new company. They can be rotated on a one-year on, one-year off, system.

INVESTORS

The best of the positions to be in if you can make the correct investments. Always use companies, ideally offshore, to own your investments. This way you have, legitimately, no tax exposure on your capital profits. Have nothing in your own name; this way the Government finds it difficult to steal from you. Always aim to do business through a corporate vehicle.

The first step in becoming wealthy is to take control of your expenditure. Everyone during their life has at least £1,000,000 flow into their pocket and the difference between those who become wealthy and those who remain poor is the amount that stays there. If you wish to build wealth you must first make sure that you live within your income and that you do not fall into debt.

The rules of becoming wealthy are:

1. Never spend more than you have as income.

2. Never borrow to spend.

3. Always save some of your income.

4. Have two businesses; one that you work at to pay for your day-to-day living expenses, and one that is your long-term wealth builder.

5. Buy a flat, improve it and then sell it and repeat the process. Your home should always be a part of your wealth-creation process.

6. Remember to apply the 'asset test' to everything you buy. See below.

7. Unless you have special knowledge on a company do not buy shares. However, when you can afford it, run a call option, or several call options on the FTSE index. See below.

8. Run a gold option in a similar manner to your FTSE options. (Paper money is always destroyed by the Governments that issue it – it can't keep from stealing) but gold endures. (The gold coins issued by the Byzantine Empire around 1100 AD were still in use, at full value, 800 years later! The US dollar,

which had endured without protection for 100 years, lost 95% of its value by the end of the 2000 after the US Government set up the Federal Reserve Bank to 'protect its value' in 1913!)

9. Aim to acquire property assets in the London area that will produce both an income and a capital profit. See below.

10. Always use companies to hold your business activities, and assets, once you have moved beyond being employed by someone else, with your own home. See below.

11. Make yourself financially literate. Watch Bloomberg or CNBC for at least half an hour each day. Know what the stock and currency markets are doing. Try to work out what you think is moving them. Try to predict where they will go tomorrow and why. Read the financial editorial of a decent newspaper daily.

Why London Property?

Well, as Mark Twain is reputed to have said, 'They aren't making any more land'. The population in Britain is growing at roughly fifty per cent per annum faster than the supply of housing and with the London area receiving an ever-increasing section of the population. People are moving to London from all over England and it is the preferred destination of immigrants: high demand and low supply.

On call options initially, buy a two-month 'call' and then 'roll' it (or them) after one month for a further month out, repeating the process every month. When the option becomes 'in the money', take advice from your broker, and sell against it. This way you retain stock market exposure without any of the downside risk and on upward market moves can take in income. Do not gear-up when selling against your 'long' (purchased) position. The revenue from the sale of your 'short' (sold) position should always generate enough income to finance the rollout of your 'long' position and give you a profit. If it won't, then don't do it.

THE ASSET TEST: this is a test you should apply before buying anything. Expenditure is either upon consumables (food, clothes, medicines etc.) or capital goods. A capital good is that which will produce a profit, or an income, and is an asset, whereas a capital good that produces no return, or is a cost, is a liability. A good example of a capital good that is a liability is a car. Another is a second home that produces neither a net income nor an after-tax profit, greater than the costs of buying and owning it.

Wealth Rules of Thumb

THE 30 TEST

In my experience, if a person has not been successful in creating material wealth by the time they are thirty, they will never become independently wealthy.

ME AS A BENCHMARK

In my own case, by the time I was twenty-eight, I had established my own successful business employing ten people. I had become professionally qualified by studying in the evenings (diploma in marketing as well as becoming semi-qualified as an accountant and gaining an HNC in business studies at London University). I had acquired two properties; one I lived in and one I rented to Sabena Airways. I had enabled my wife to cease working for others and become employed at home looking after the accounts of my business. I had taught her to drive and bought her a new car for cash. I supported my mother enabling her to cease working. I had bought a new Jaguar V12 E-type, in cash, for myself.
By the time I was thirty I had moved to a 24–acre estate in Hampshire. I employed sixty staff in two companies, and my wife and I drove matching Bentleys.

CARS AND CLOTHES

These are good indicators of the ability of people to manage their lives and businesses. If they are not clean and tidy then their owner is, generally, incapable of running a successful business.

PARASITES

Most people do not look to work to create wealth but to attach themselves to someone who does, and then 'transfer' that wealth to themselves. Like the Government they consider that, although they are not clever enough to create wealth, they are cleverer than the wealth-creator in spending it!

ACCOUNTANTS AND SOLICITORS

They are usually commercially incompetent and should never to be relied upon or trusted, except when absolutely necessary, especially in matters of commercial judgement or where something has to be achieved.

MY SYSTEM

I have used various note-taking systems over the years in an attempt to control the various activities in my life. I have found the biggest problem has always been having people keep to their undertakings. People will, in general, say whatever they feel fits the moment and then choose to follow through with their commitments only if it fits with their later best interests – and sometimes not even then!

Over the years I have experienced particular problems in this regard with accountants who seem especially afflicted with the problem of promising and not implementing!

By a process of evolution I have arrived at the following system which does not prevent the problem, but which does allow you to control it, and identify those people, and areas, that are dangerous to your interests. It also shows you the people who keep to their word and in whom your experience shows you can have confidence.

The four components of my system are:
1. A page-a-day diary.
2. A 'jobs' list.
3. An alphabetically indexed A4 file.
4. Files upon each company or subject who I am dealing with.

The diary is the foundation of my system insofar as it controls my time. I break each page down as follows: down the left-hand side I list any appointments against their times on a 24-hour clock; I use only surnames. In the centre I list jobs that I must progress or complete that day; and on the right-hand top side of the page I list phone calls I must make – when made successfully I cross them out, or, if expecting a return call I tick them and then carry them forward to the bottom of the next day's page if not returned by the end of the day.

Diary example:

	APPOINTMENTS	ACTION	PHONE
09.00	Jones		Watkins
			Smith
11.00	Wallace		
		Berkeley Ct. – inspect.	
		C. card – insure	
13.00		Car – service	Jones

MY JOBS LIST

My jobs list is a continuing list of all the jobs that I aim to complete, but do not yet have definite timings that can be transferred to my diary. I review this list each evening for the next day. I list jobs by subject and then action, for example: car – service.

INDEX FILE

While my diary is the foundation, or the 'feet' of my system, the index file is the 'spine'. Everything you do, normally, is done with, or through, a person, and this file is my control, indexed under his or her surname, of what each person has agreed with me. This file travels everywhere with me.

I always take notes at meetings, then, at the end of each meeting I summarise the outcome: with each person I discuss their tasks to be done and when they are to be completed by. I then let them see me writing this down and agree a meeting time to review progress – which I then diarise, of course.

The reason this system is indexed on the person's surname is because you may have one person handling several different matters for you, and you do not need the whole file on each subject if you know the specific item to be achieved. The other advantage to having a summary in this form is whenever you speak to that person, say by phone, you can turn to his or her page and you will have an immediate 'position' on your affairs with that person. You also have the facility of being able to make notes of any subject that comes to mind concerning that person.

I have been amazed at how often 'professionals', particularly accountants, do not do as they have promised. (It appears that as they usually have a lot of detailed responsibilities that their clients are uninformed about, they can rely on their clients forgetting the promises they have made to them).

At each review meeting with a person I rewrite the summary list, with an up-to-date summary of objectives and times. I then file the old list.

FILES

I run two types of files; one on each person and one on each subject. In the person file, I put the old summaries and in the subject file I keep the relevant paperwork. I aim to review all subject files at least once per month.

This system is a superb way of keeping on top of your affairs, and in my experience will always give you the best position in managing your affairs, if you use it. As with all systems, however, it will only work if you *make* it work for you! Of all the many systems I have used over the years this one works best of all. However, I must emphasise again, that it has to be made to work and to obtain the best from it you have to keep to its disciplines.

Peace Of Mind

'I joined the Foreign Legion to forget,' he said. 'Forget what?' I said. 'I don't know, I've forgotten!' he said.

Summary

Peace of mind is a state of mind where you feel comfortable with the position you are in, in life. It is a state of mental equilibrium where you feel in balance with what you are, with what you would like to be, where you are with where you would like to have been, and who you are with whom you would have liked to be. It is the acceptance of past mistakes and past successes as part of the process of living, feeling mild regret for the mistakes, and mild pleasure at the successes, but being neither haunted for the former nor jubilant over the latter.

Peace of mind can be achieved by an acceptance by yourself, of yourself, an acceptance of your humanity with a sense of compassion for your mistakes of the past, and a feeling of gentle accomplishment in your previous successes. Neither your past mistakes, nor successes, should be taken as an excuse for failing to continue in trying to achieve now and in the future. It is not an excuse for complacency or slothfulness. Peace of mind carries with it a determination to continue to progress, while learning from the past, without being burdened by it.

Remember, the successful people in life make many mistakes, because in trying to succeed a person will often make mistakes. It is only those people who do not attempt to succeed who do not fail. There is a Chinese saying, 'If you never want to lose at chess don't play', and many people apply this approach to just about their whole life. They never fail on the big things of life because they never attempt them in the first place. Their passage through life is an unmarked event – even by themselves.

In an ideal world we would correctly evaluate each situation and opportunity, avoiding those situations that we later regret and exploiting more fully those with great potential. Unfortunately, however, we sometimes lack the knowledge to do this and we either embark upon a wrong venture or fail to capitalise properly upon a good opportunity. Where this occurs it is important to release the past. Keep the experience and the acquired knowledge for future use but accept our own humanness in our mistake and move on. The world very rarely notices your mistakes, or lost opportunities, and the only person keeping them alive is yourself. Let it go. Forgive yourself. Allow yourself your own humanness. Maintain a period of mourning if you require it but be aware that you are doing this for yourself and the world does not require it. On the other hand, do not consider that you have a licence to behave without thought, or consideration, for others and the consequences of your behaviour. It is simply that the past is past. Having made a mistake or missed an opportunity, which cannot be undone, you are now in a new reality with its own challenges and opportunities and you should adjust to this.

Equally, when you have a large success it's important to maintain a balanced perspective on it. The success may be because of your efforts and plans or may be because of good fortune. It is important, as Rudyard Kipling says, 'To treat those two impostors Triumph and Disaster both the same' and, while increasing your understanding, not let them change your approach to life in a manner that spoils your ability to continue to make progress.

Peace of mind comes from an understanding that all that you do, and aim to do, is intended to benefit yourself and never to harm others. It may be that your actions do cause detriment to others but this must never be your intention. If, in the achievement of your aims, you may cause harm to others it is important to firstly consider the cost/benefit relationship between yourself and others. This is a highly subjective evaluation in many situations as it is often very difficult to correctly evaluate the full consequences of some actions. This 'hazard analysis' should be examined wherever possible before embarking upon a new venture. While it would be nice to say that one should never do anything that can cause detriment to others, this is a recipe for inaction as one can always find some possible way in which some other person may be disadvantaged by an action. The important considerations are, firstly, that the proposed course of action is of real benefit to yourself and not being done to harm someone else; and, secondly, that you have thought through the action and weighed the benefit to yourself against any detriment to others, and you believe that your benefit will, in retrospect, justify their detriment.

For clarification I should include, for example, a situation where a soldier is required to kill his country's enemies. His main aim is, ostensibly, to harm someone else, while, in reality, it is to serve his country. His refusal to carry out his duties could cost him his life and thus it is in his own interests to harm others. As Mr George Orwell writes, 'Civilised men sleep well in their beds at night because rough men stand ready to do violence on their behalf'.

It is my experience that actions which are carried out by intelligent people, with the sole aim of harming others, cause those perpetrators of harm quite severe distress in later time. I believe that this is because the negative nature of such actions causes a thinking person distress because of empathy with the person hurt. The inequity of causing material pain, without any corresponding substantial benefit, for a thinking person, causes distress. He is unable to justify his actions to himself and his empathy with his victim haunts him.

I would, at this stage, like to make the point that education is not intelligence. I have met many educated fools and several, very intelligent, uneducated people. Intelligence is the ability to process information well, while education is simply information and its relationships. The mere possession of information does not guarantee its intelligent use. An intelligent person can do a lot with the little information at his disposal. While an unintelligent person, even though equipped with a great deal of information, can achieve little.

An unintelligent person does not appear, in my experience, to suffer any remorse over his harmful actions to others. My experience of negative actions, taken by people without any apparent benefit to themselves, has led me to the view that one should always presume that others will attempt pointless harm, unless one has evidence that they will not. Do not depend upon the generosity of others and expect them to act negatively. Preparing for the worst enhances peace of mind. Expecting a person to act in his own best interests is a reasonable start in understanding what and why someone will do something. However, be prepared for them to act negatively towards you even if it is of no benefit to them. (See my notes on 'What Drives Everyone?')

In conclusion, peace of mind comes from a positive acceptance of oneself, warts and all, with an acceptance, also, that life is about effort, with failure being a natural part of success.

Correct Eating

'But Doctor,' said the rather overweight lady, 'I've been following the diet you prescribed for me for over a month now and I still haven't lost any weight.'

'I don't understand it,' said the Doctor, 'this diet has always worked with my patients until now. Are you sure you've been following it strictly?'

'Oh yes,' came the reply,' I always eat it as soon as I've had my normal meal!'

Summary
To obtain the best from life you have to treat your body as the amazing machine it is and give it the care, maintenance, and fuel it best works with.

I believe that your diet should consist mainly of a wide range of fruits, vegetables, nuts, and wholegrains with fish and chicken. Eat eggs once or twice per week. Eat red meat – including bacon and sausages – only if you have to, in great moderation, and no more than once or twice per week.

Avoid milk and milk products (butter and cheese) like the plague. I believe that milk and milk products are the main cause of several cancers, particularly breast cancer, and that girls, especially, should never drink or eat them. Milk is a great food for baby cows but even grown cows will not drink it – so why humans should believe they can is beyond my comprehension!

Drink filtered water daily; drink coffee in moderation, no more than two cups per day and then never after midday, unless you really need the stimulus (e.g. for an exam.). Drink weak tea without milk or sugar and never after six o'clock in the evening. If you must drink alcohol then do so in moderation, three glasses of wine or its equivalent as a maximum per day and do not drink alcohol every second day.

All of the evidence suggests that smoking causes cancers of the lungs, mouth, throat, nose, and just about everywhere else. It also causes poverty. Smoking, as with drugs, tattoos, fatness and facial hair (in men!) is a way you can tell the sort of person you don't want to be or know. This appears prejudiced, and probably is, but it's one of my rules-of-thumb that has worked consistently well for me.

If your diet is largely fruit and vegetables and you stay away from excess carbohydrates, such as in bread and potatoes, it is highly unlikely that you will be overweight. If you follow this eating approach and maintain an exercise programme that includes three sessions of running per week, your weight should never be a problem. In my experience the most effective way to control weight is through additional aerobic exercise while carefully cutting back on carbohydrate consumption. Rapid weight loss is to be avoided as it rarely stays off. It is better to gradually adjust your lifestyle until you reach a balance between exercise, diet, recreation, and work that you can comfortably maintain.

VITAMINS

I have taken a selection of vitamins supplements for most of my life and continue to do so, taking daily, in cold-pressed oil capsules, vitamins E, B and cod liver oil, although I am unsure as to whether they have any beneficial effect. There is, however, one supplement that I do believe is amazing and that is Echinacea capsules (from Boots) that I have found virtually miraculous in preventing and curing colds and flues. I recommend that one capsule should be taken daily for a week, every second week. If you have signs of a cold coming on, take two capsules three times per day for three days, and then one capsule three times per day for a further three days.

KEEPING FIT

Summary
Fitness is exactly what it says, being fit for a purpose. So, therefore, to determine if you are sufficiently fit you first of all have to define what it is you wish to be fit for. The fitness requirement of a bureaucrat is very different to that of a

professional athlete, and even different athletes have different levels and types of fitness.

One consideration to fitness is that there is a foundation level of fitness that every able person should achieve and maintain, unless they become disabled in some way that prevents them from doing so. In my estimation, from the age of sixteen, every boy should be able to run a mile in six minutes, and a girl in eight minutes. Similarly, a boy should be able to bench-press his own weight and a girl half her own weight.

I believe that everyone should take an hour's exercise *at least* three times per week that should include, *as a minimum*, a one-mile run, 5 x 10 sit-ups and 5 x 10 push-ups.

Regular exercise is vital to achieve good behaviour in children, particularly teenagers from the age of thirteen to nineteen. It is almost impossible to over-exercise children, especially boys, and, in my experience, an hour's varied exercise each day, as long as it is balanced with eight to ten hours' sleep, will ensure that they behave in a calm and reasonable manner.

In my belief, the best exercise programme for children is to enrol them in a gymnastics class, three times per week, from the age of three until, at least, sixteen and then enrol them into a good karate or kick-boxing club. From around fourteen years of age, there should be a gradual introduction to weight training, two sessions per week, starting with very light weights, and spending no more than thirty minutes per session.

Football, volleyball, water polo, squash, karate, boxing, tennis, and cricket are all great sports and should be encouraged. Rugby and American Football are extremely dangerous and carry no short or long-term virtue. Horse riding is equally dangerous and is pretentious and irrelevant in today's world. Students of martial arts should train regularly and compete once or twice but no more, no matter how successful in competition. Repeated punches to the head do real damage and does not improve the student's long-term academic ability!

I have come to the belief that regular running is a very important part of overall fitness, even when other programmes are followed. I believe that running three times per week should be incorporated into a fitness regime from the age of five, of course, starting with small distances and, if possible, built into some form of game for the child. By the age of twelve, a child should be jogging one mile three times per week and by the age of sixteen this should be one to two miles per session. Running is a great way to warm-up for an exercise session.

Children should be introduced to water from the age of one year and they should be swimming and practising regularly from the age of three; it could save their life. Water polo is a superb sport for building stamina and should be encouraged if the child is interested in it.

Exercise should always fit into your life. You should ensure that your exercise programme is one that you can easily keep to. If you find yourself unable to exercise at least three times per week, then you must adjust your life and priorities to allow you to do so. By failing to exercise regularly I have frequently made myself ill, when I have attempted to resume the same level of exercise as I felt I was capable of (and obviously wasn't!). Your body will adjust to your exercise regime if your programme is sensible to your lifestyle and appropriate to your physical capacities. Make time for regular exercise, the investment is well worth the effort and any sacrifices you may have to make. Regular exercise allows you to extend your life span, keeps you more healthy, reduces illness, increases your stamina, allows you to work and study better, makes you more tolerant and balanced, and generally adds enormously to your quality of life.

Avoid over-exercising, unless you are a professional athlete, under continual professional coaching and medical supervision, working to a competition or a target, otherwise over-exercise will only harm you. Professional athletes also have regular controlled breaks and do not work continually to a maximum standard. Exercise has to be balanced with rest and even professional athletes have a short professional life and their active sport does not occupy all of their life overall.

Understanding, Measurement and Balance

Summary
In understanding anything, I have found that it is necessary to appreciate the difference between the two fundamental means of measurement – the relative and the absolute.

Relative means what it says – that is, how one item relates to another. For example, I'm taller than Ruth but shorter than George.

Absolute, defines how something is in finite terms. For example, I am six foot tall; George is six foot two inches tall.

It's often useful to use a combination of both measures to establish an accurate picture. For example, in assessing my children's performance in a school examination I would always ask for both their mark and class position. This would allow me to assess their true performance, as a 5 out of 20 mark, at first view, looks awful, but when the rest of the class obtained 4 out of 20 it looks excellent.

The reason why I consider it important to include in my notes this simple observation on measurement is, because on many occasions I've found myself confused or misled by having the wrong set of parameters to measure, and therefore deal correctly with a situation. Conversely, I have often found myself able to deal correctly with situations when I have identified the correct form of measurement.

Watch out for words like 'more', 'do better', 'enough', 'contribute', 'help', as too often they are verbal tools being used to prevent you identifying exactly what is expected of you. Conversely, your ability to understand and use these two simple concepts will allow you to avoid harm and often manage situations to your advantage.

Wherever possible in my notes I attempt to define my concepts in the correct relevant term and where possible, in both.

BALANCE

This is the process of maintaining the relationship between power and responsibility, or, cost and benefit.

In life it is vital to correctly assess the balance of these two factors in any situation. Wherever possible never accept a situation where you have to assume the responsibility for achieving an objective, without being given the corresponding power to control the causal circumstances. Similarly, never accept that you should pay for something unless you can choose what it is you have to pay for, and what benefit you will receive from it.

An obvious example of the latter is having a joint bank account with someone who does not contribute but can withdraw. A situation of this nature is very dangerous for the responsible, or paying, person. They have the burden to either ensure an achievement or pay for a cost and it is imperative that they retain control over the circumstances under which that aim is to be achieved or cost incurred.

When employing someone it is important to maintain this balance in their employment, making sure that the employee has adequate power to achieve his work goal and no latitude to misuse his position. Similarly, when employed, it is necessary to ensure that your employer gives you the resources to achieve your work aims.

There are many examples of systems within our society that lack this balance and consequently are causing grave inequities and tremendous social damage. Examples are:

OUR SOCIAL SYSTEM: encourages those people who are least capable of caring for children to have children, while discouraging those who are most capable from having them.

OUR POLICING SYSTEM: is designed not to discourage and prevent but to encourage crime. (This has been achieved by removing officers from regular street patrols, thereby discouraging crime by their presence, and instead, putting them in police stations or cars and responding only when crime has occurred.)

OUR LABOUR LAWS: employers are expected to produce wealth as well as being responsible for the behaviour of their employees, without having the corresponding powers to freely choose and discipline their employees.

OUR IMMIGRATION POLICIES: aimed at encouraging illegal and disruptive immigration.

OUR TRADE UNION SYSTEM: assists in the destruction of individual freedoms as well as businesses and entire industries.

OUR POLICIES ON INDUSTRIAL AND COMMERCIAL DEVELOPMENT: succeed in destroying existing and discouraging new industries.

INCOME TAX

The biggest fraud is our income tax system. This is another example of a similarly unbalanced structure, where those who are forced to contribute have no real power to control the expenditure. The wealth-creators are doing what the bureaucrats can't do – creating wealth – and they are not allowed to spend the wealth they have created. Those bureaucrats who are incapable of creating wealth believe that their inability to create somehow qualifies them to spend the wealth created by others!

Truth and Beauty

'Have you heard about the latest utility knickers?' asked one British soldier of another, after reading a letter from home.

'No, what are they?' asked his trenchmate.

The reply came, 'One Yank and they're off!'

Summary
While the truth is always beautiful, that which is often considered beautiful is not always the truth.

I believe that the truth, no matter how unwelcome it may be, is always beautiful because it is correct and may be worked with, whereas, an illusion cannot be built upon as it is, by its nature, fundamentally untrue and therefore unstable. When facing any situation, or opportunity, the aim should always be to establish the truth of the component factors as it is only upon the true realities of a situation that one may build or progress.

For example, if your work is not up to standard, an accurate assessment by your boss can be of great assistance in helping you improve your performance, or, at least establishing for you that the employment you are in is not for you. Of course when dealing with the truth several factors need to be considered, for example, delivery of the truth should be made in such a way as to keep it in context. A small success or failure should not be presented as a major one. Equally, the person who tells you the truth should not automatically become identified as your friend or enemy. It is always important in assessing the value of a truth, that one considers the motives of the person imparting the information.

By maintaining an open mind on information, and being prepared to not 'kill the messenger', bringing bad news or embracing as absolutely correct, the bringer of good, then one makes it easy to define the truth and progress from it.

While I would always maintain that the correctly delivered

truth is beautiful, the reverse is not true. Definitions of beauty are often changing, and subject to subjective judgement, in consequence they are not always true. I have always subscribed to the belief that the 'form should follow the function' and that if the appearance or design of someone, or something, failed to achieve their or its function, efficiently, then they could not be beautiful. For example, in the 1990s many young female fashion models were anaemic and looked addicted to drugs, and in consequence they failed in their portrayal as successful females. They may have been fashionable and generally considered beautiful by their contemporaries, however, I maintain that they carried no beauty as they carried no truth.

Similar arguments apply to machines, buildings, and other physical structures. Beauty, as a subjective assessment, has to be qualified by the efficiency of the way in which the object discharges its function. I would also qualify this process by the introduction of time, as what may be functional in one era may be surpassed by technology. I find, for example, old machines, which have been made technologically obsolete, still have great beauty when valued in the context of their own time and technology.

On this note, I would mention that in times of scarcity of food plump ladies were considered beautiful, whereas today, in times of abundance, even marginal female obesity is generally considered unattractive.

What Drives Everyone?

Summary
What drives everyone in life? I believe that we all have the same fundamental drive, although it often demonstrates itself differently in different people, at different times and in different societies.

You believe that you exist because you think, however, you are not sure because you may only be a dream in the mind of someone else. You need to prove to yourself that you are real. Your initial reassurance comes from your sense data – your senses of touch, sight, hearing, taste and smell. However, they only give transitory and superficial reassurance. You seek reassurance of your existence by seeing how you affect the world and people around you.

You need to confirm that others know you exist. You know that your sense data can be fraudulent and that what you feel may only be a delusion. You are aware but unsure as to what you are and how you relate to the universe around you, and while you feel that you exist, this is not enough; you need proof and not just once but continuing and increasingly more profound proof.

What is it that drives everyone? What is it that lies behind and beneath the motivation of people? What is it that makes men die for their country, accept torture rather than change their beliefs, and yet also have the ability to act against their loved ones? What motivation consistently underpins this behaviour?

I have read that man, above all else, is motivated by a desire to survive, and yet, history is filled with examples of men who have died to save others: men who have died for a belief, men who have sacrificed themselves to make an academic or religious point.

I have also read that the main drive in man is to reproduce, to ensure the survival of the species, yet we continually read of the collapsing birth rates of the civilised world, as well as seeing that many of our contemporaries are choosing not to have children, or, at most, to have one token child.

If man is not primarily motivated to survive, or to procreate, then what is his fundamental motivating drive?

It is my belief that man – the genus not the gender – is unlike any other animal, fundamentally motivated by one pressure that overrides all others, and that pressure is to prove his existence to himself. Convince a man that charging a machine-gun proves his existence then he'll do it. Convince him that he is chosen by God, and that God needs him to die to show his faith, and he'll happily do so. He is not dying for God, he is dying because he needs the feedback of seeing himself gain recognition of his existence, and he believes that this act will give this. ('Father, why hast thou forsaken me?')

Convince a man that he proves his existence by running a mile in under four minutes and he'll work as hard as he can to achieve this – to the point of crippling himself. Convince a man that wealth, popularity, academic success, or political correctness is how he proves his existence then he will live his life to achieve this.

Where there is an absence of a focus of proof, then man will randomly search to establish some form of feedback that feels to him as though it proves his existence. This can manifest itself in a wide variety of ways. Violence is common and acts as a temporary relief insofar as the perpetrator feels a strong proof of his existence, by observing the relationship between his action and the often, dramatic, consequences. The attraction of violent proofs is that they are often easily achieved and give a strong demonstration, whereas other, more positive consequences are far harder to achieve and take much longer to effect.

In understanding that we are primarily motivated in our actions to prove our existence then we have an extremely valuable tool in understanding, not only why others do things, but also what motivates ourselves. We can also see that we have a powerful tool in developing our children by ensuring that as we understand behaviour for what it fundamentally is, we can encourage positive behaviour by strong recognition, while punishing negative with a withdrawal of recognition.

As we mature, the audience that we seek recognition from alters. Initially this audience is our mother, this then becomes our parents (although the mother normally dominates) the father may transitorily become more prominent, then siblings, then school friends, followed by work friends. Then, as we have our own children, our audience moves back to our family.

This understanding of human nature also explains why the actions of any human group is focused upon their peer group and not upon their announced audience. For example, politicians and state employees are reluctantly made accountable to the electorate, and entertainers prefer the high opinion of their peers to those of their real, paying audience.

What is the Nature of Life?

A vicar was having his breakfast and had just thickly buttered and blackberry-jammed a crisp piece of toast when the telephone rang and, as he stood to answer the phone, he dropped the toast! The toast tumbled through the air towards the beautiful new beige carpet his wife had just, that week, had newly laid!

The toast, having somersaulted half-a-dozen times landed on the unjammed side! No damage was done! And the vicar was, after answering the phone, even able to eat the toast!

This bothered the vicar all day and he discussed this occurrence with his wife that evening. She too was unable to offer an explanation and so he went to see his bishop. The bishop was lost for words and arranged to pass the matter on to the archbishop who, in turn, after much thought passed the matter to the synod. The synod, after days of debate passed down the answer to the vicar and it was, 'You buttered and jammed the wrong side of the toast.'

Summary

What is the nature of life? By this I mean how does one define the underlying foundation to all aspects of all life upon this planet? Is it goodness, wickedness, the desire to survive, to reproduce?

Answer: I believe that life has two aspects: the physical and the metaphysical, and that in the physical aspect the one consistent factor in all forms of life is in its nature to exploit. I therefore maintain that, the nature of physical life is exploitative. While in the metaphysical aspect I believe that Sod's Law prevails and that the metaphysical aspect of life is ironic.

Lesson: therefore knowing this how should we live?

Answer: eighty per cent defensively, and twenty per cent aggressively. Never take life for granted, never relax completely. Always expect the unexpected and even then be sure that life will always, probably, surprise you – unless you expect to be surprised!

Explanation: if we view life as being similar in form to an iceberg, with the small visible section protruding above the water resembling the physical aspect of life, and the unseen majority of the iceberg corresponding to the metaphysical. Our experience of life appears to be purely subject to physical, material cause and effects, yet most people would accept that events often suggest an other than physical dimension.

I believe that physical events occur within, or rest upon, a metaphysical context, and although I cannot explain how the metaphysical directly relates to the physical world, I can, from experience, deduce that one has to prepare oneself for irony in all situations. The metaphysical nature of life is not necessarily malevolent and there may be occasions when, should one drop a slice of thickly buttered and jammed toast, then it may land jam side up. However, this will only occur when one is sure that it will land jam side down! In all other cases it will always land with the jam side down! Particularly so when one really needs it to land jam side up!

All life forms are driven to exploit the opportunities and weaknesses that life offers. The entropic nature of the universe, its natural winding down, is the context within which the exploitative nature of life forms manifests itself.

The structure within which the Government serves its citizens is really one where the Government exploits the desires of its citizens for certain services in return for compliance in forfeiting a proportion of their wealth and freedom. This is normally without a competitive benchmark to establish the reasonableness of these costs. Similarly, albeit in a more direct and honest manner, companies exploit their customers' needs and wants by offering goods and services in exchange for money. In the process of free competition the customer can at least ensure that he is obtaining the best relative deal available at any given time.

Animals exploit their environment. Remove a predator from an area and watch how the other species grow. Plants exploit their environment, leave a patch of ground untended and watch how quickly weeds – plants you don't want there – grow.

Customers exploit companies by buying the best deal at the

time – the customer refuses to consider the best interests of the company at the time of purchase – unless it's in his interests to do so. In which case he is, again, exploiting the market place and supplying the company to his own best interests.

Be indiscriminately generous and see how quickly people will take your generosity. Create a 'welfare system' and see how quickly dependents will grow. If you wish to justify the existence of a bureaucracy then create a welfare system that needs a bureaucracy to service it. Pretty soon your welfare system and its bureaucracy will destroy the originating society.

In relationships, both business and personal, partners exploit each other's needs and wants. This is natural and good, however, it is important to maintain a healthy balance between what you give and what you receive. In both business and personal relationships this balance has to be mutually beneficial. The salary or remuneration you receive for working should reflect the relationship you agreed – employee, director, equal partner, teaboy – time, energy, thought, and contribution you make compared to what you could earn elsewhere, while considering where your occupation could lead you to in the future. Similarly, as an employer/business associate you should consider both what you are receiving compared to that which you are giving. Both as an employer and as an employee you should look to give as well as receive if you wish to have the relationship work. Exploitation can be best achieved by ensuring that while you are not being over-exploited you also ensure that you are making a valuable needed and appreciated contribution.

In personal relationships the principle is the same. You should always look to ensure that while making a meaningful and appreciated contribution to your partner, that you are not taken for granted and that your partner is also contributing in a significant and meaningful manner to your own life. The relationship should also be one that has positive growth potential, for and from, both parties. You should never be the one who is not growing or with someone who is not prepared to make the effort to themselves grow.

Compassionate as you may be, it is in the nature of life that the weak, particularly the weak who will not help themselves, perish. If you wish your relationship to prosper then you must accept the responsibility of defending and promoting yourself and your interests both as an individual and within your partnership.

What a Girl Should Look For in a Man

Summary
This is what I have found works and brings happiness to both partners in a relationship.

I suggest my daughter should look for a man who:

1. HAS A CAREER

Not just a job – a career is for life; it gives him purpose and focus and he and his family security – it can be as a plumber, builder, businessman or a lawyer, and even, but only if absolutely necessary, a civil servant.

2. COMES FROM A PROPER HOME

The sort of home that you would like to have. People generally behave as they were brought up – the family he is from will be the subconscious model he will work to repeat.

3. YOU HAVE A BETTER EDUCATION THAN HIM

This keeps him interested and on his toes! Life is more fun and he has someone to turn to for advice.

4. LOVES YOU MORE THAN YOU LOVE HIM!

5. IS FROM THE SAME ETHNIC AND PHILOSOPHICAL GROUPS AS YOU

Don't waste your life trying to alter someone, because by the time you meet them, it's too late for them to change.

6. WANTS CHILDREN

Firstly, I want grandchildren, and secondly, anyone who doesn't want kids is faulted and one of nature's dead ends.

7. DOES NOT HAVE FACIAL HAIR

A beard, moustache, or long sideburns always shows a man is hiding something.

8. IS FIT AND CLEAN

Apart from being civilised to live with, if they look after their body they'll probably look after their partner and family.

9. IS SMARTLY DRESSED BUT NOT FASHIONABLE

Any man with extreme dress, earrings, tattoos or a hairstyle or sorts, and thinks only of appearances and the trivia of life, and not achievements and his family, has very little depth and there's no future with or for him.

What a Man Should Look For in a Woman

MALE MATURITY

When I was 14, all I had was spots but I hoped that one day I would have a girlfriend.

When I was 16 I still had the spots but I found a girlfriend, however, there was no passion. So I decided I needed a passionate girl with a zest for life.

In college I dated a passionate girl, but she was too emotional. Everything was an emergency; she was a drama queen, cried all the time and threatened suicide. So I decided I needed a girl with stability.

When I was 25 I found a very stable girl but she was boring. She was totally predictable and never got excited about anything. Life became so dull that I decided that I needed a girl with some excitement.

When I was 28 I found an exciting girl, but I couldn't keep up with her. She rushed from one thing to another, never settling on anything. She did mad impetuous things and made me miserable as often as happy. She was great fun initially and very energetic, but directionless. So I decided to find a girl with some real ambition.

When I turned 31, I found a smart ambitious girl with her feet planted firmly on the ground and married her. She was so ambitious that she divorced me and took everything I owned.

I am now 40, have lost the spots, and I am looking for a girl with very big tits!

I Suggest That my Son Should Look for a Girl:

1. WHO HAS A CAREER BUT WANTS A FAMILY

This makes her confident in life and able to look after your family should anything happen to you.

2. COMES FROM A PROPER HOME

The home she comes from will be her model for the home she will build with you.

3. IS BETTER EDUCATED THAN HIM

Also, if it's possible for you to assess it, also more intelligent. This way she is an asset and resource who can build with you, assist you and have valuable insight when required. She also should have an interest in, or at least an awareness of, life. This gives you both something to share when the first blush of romance has worn off.

4. YOU LOVE HER MORE THAN SHE LOVES YOU!

This is a particularly tricky one for you to assess, however, with this bias it keeps you interested. Obviously you have to ensure that you are not exploited, however, if she is a family person this is unlikely.

5. ETHNIC GROUP

Is from the same ethnic and philosophical group as you. Don't waste your life trying to alter the way someone is because by the time you meet them it's too late for them to change.

6. WANTS CHILDREN

Firstly, I want grandchildren and, secondly, anyone who doesn't is faulted and one of nature's dead ends.

7. LOOKS AFTER HER APPEARANCE

Personal hygiene and where she lives is important. How she looks matters – to her as well as to you. She should have a good, easy to maintain, appearance, and not just look good after she has made a big effort. How she lives is how she will look after your home.

8. EXERCISE

Takes regular, sensible, exercise and looks after her body. Only drinks moderately (if at all) and doesn't smoke or take drugs.

9. DRESS

Is nicely dressed but not too fashionable. Does not have tattoos, piercings or high-maintenance hairstyles or clothes. Appearance has to be important to her but not to the exclusion of everything else.

10. DICTION AND TONE

Speaks nicely, and does not shout, swear, or become violent, when she is under normal domestic pressure.

What You Should Aim For in Life – and Why

Summary
'More than enough is a burden'. There are only two things of which a person can never have too much of: true knowledge and true wealth.

In my experience, the possession of everything, other than true wealth and true knowledge, carries with it a real cost. For example, the ownership of a business carries with it substantial burdens; as an unpaid mechanism of social change; the inequitable burden of being responsible for the actions of your staff without having the corresponding power to control them; the requirement to act as an unpaid collector of taxes; the role as a 'Baddie' in society because of the reality that the nature of a business requires it to attempt to make profits, and profit-motivated actions are generally considered to be bad in today's society.

The ownership of property – all forms – has to be carefully

considered to establish whether or not it is an asset and part of the true wealth concept. For example, particularly in Latin Europe, the ownership of property is anything other than true wealth, and should only be accepted if there are other benefits, as opposed to holding property as part of your assets. For example, the costs of buying and selling property ('in' and 'out' costs) in Spain and France are around 40%, roughly 15% to buy and 25% to sell, with substantial other financial considerations in the ownership of the property, including residential, taxation and maintenance costs. Generally speaking, it is far more profitable to rent rather than buy property in Spain and France. Although depending upon your personal circumstances, this may not be your main concern, however, as a simple financial exercise I have never found a reason to buy as opposed to rent, as yet.

Furnishings are another consideration; do you obtain benefit from owning more than you need? If you do then own, however, in most situations people have very little utility or pleasure in their possessions, and rather than being of benefit these possessions are a burden. Possessions need to be maintained, ask yourself before acquiring any possession whether or not you are happy to pay the cost, in money, time, and effort, in maintaining a possession, and if you believe that you will receive the benefit relative to the total cost of buying and maintaining that possession.

Similar arguments attach themselves to clothes. We all enjoy a choice of clothes, however, clothes are easy to buy and forget. Look at your wardrobe from time-to-time and you'll be amazed at the money wasted and the clothes unused.

A further area of more being less is personal adornment and habits. Anything that costs you money, effort, or time, and does not really increase your knowledge or wealth, is a waste. Good everyday examples are, smoking, drugs, excessive drinking, tattoos, body piercings, fashionable non-functionable clothing and computer time-filling games. 'More than enough is a burden', is very relevant here, any one of the items on this list is a burden, and two are a crucifixion!

Poor people generally are poor because they choose to be. They choose to smoke, drink, take drugs, have tattoos and body piercings and, generally, instead of saving and investing their surplus income, spend it on irrelevant expenditure. They usually are paying off large debts at excessive rates of interest. The debts being entered into to buy goods for which they had no real need or from which they obtained no real benefit.

True wealth is that which carries a benefit materially greater than the cost of ownership and which can also be easily transacted – sold or exchanged – without penalty. For example, money, shares, bonds, long options, property in jurisdictions where there are no penalties or unreasonable costs associated with its ownership, all fit into the category of true wealth.

True knowledge is harder to define and is probably more easily defined by what it is not as opposed to what it is. It is not true knowledge to remember the name of every pop idol current on the world stage, unless that knowledge is relevant to your business or professional career. Similarly, the memorising of a telephone directory, or ten packs of playing cards is pointless unless it carries with it some commercial, scientific, or social benefit. True knowledge will always, at some point, carry with it some utility. The proof of true knowledge is what can be done with it and the laborious accumulation of irrelevant facts has, rarely, any value.

True knowledge falls within how to advance man's health, wealth, or understanding of the universe. True knowledge is not simply the ability to remember large amounts of data, computers can do that, true knowledge is in understanding and the correct use of that understanding.

What to Teach Your Children

Summary
I would suggest that you teach your children the following simple rules and make their, and your, lives easier, nicer, and more successful.

1. 'Manners maketh the man'. Teach your children when to say please and thank you, to you, their brothers and sisters, and to others, in particular to other adults.

2. That the most important thing they have in life is their family and each other.

   With siblings, a child has a network which can assist it throughout its life and which it, in turn, is obliged to assist when needed. In a world where, increasingly, it is difficult and perilous to trust either the State, or other people, having a brother or a sister that you can turn to for honest advice, and assistance, is a tremendous advantage. Any study of the Rich List will show that the vast majority of self-made rich people have done so, as one of two or more brothers or sisters, who have co-operated in building a business and subsequent wealth.

3. To return anything taken or used to its correct location and to keep their room, bathroom and possessions in clean and correct order.

4. To shower, both in the morning and evening, every day, and to always leave the bathroom clean and tidy every time they use it.

5. To understand that to obtain the best from life they have a responsibility to constructively contribute to situations, while retaining awareness that if their contribution is not reciprocated then, after making a reasonable attempt to contribute, they should not continue and waste their efforts.

6. The nature of God. See my notes.

7. The importance of regular and proper exercise.

8. Correct eating. See my notes.

9. Correct studying. See my notes.

10. A total distrust of the State and all of its bureaucracies.

11. To think carefully before they act. See my 80/20 rules notes.

12. To always behave in a pleasant, polite, and constructive manner, unless attacked. This minimises the excuse for an attack and allows constructive relationships with similar, constructive people.

13. To see everyone as a potential threat until they are sure that they are not, however, to act as though they treat everyone as a friend unless they are known to be an enemy. The reason for this slight deception is, that by adopting this approach you allow benevolent people to come into your life easily while still retaining a cautionary approach and an ability to react to an unfriendly act.

14. By behaving in a pleasant and polite manner at all times they do not lose the ability to take strong defensive action. Polite behaviour in the face of aggression disconcerts the aggressor yet does not prevent strong retaliation.

15. The dangers of acting upon impulse and to never let other people manipulate them into actions they do not wish to take. To never respond to provocative comments or actions in a manner that they would not normally take after suitable consideration.

16. That the best way to make progress in anything is to work to do it correctly, and not just quickly. If you focus upon learning to do something properly, with practise, you will then be able to do it quickly. However, if you focus upon doing something quickly you will probably never learn to do it at all!

17. The symbols that help a person to define what is and what is not, a 'proper man'. See my notes.

18. To read and understand the poem 'If' by Rudyard Kipling, *1984* by George Orwell, and *Fit for Life* by Harvey Diamond.

19. Every day to read the headlines, at least, in one good newspaper and to know where the FTSE Index is.

20. To know how to use I Ching to find answers to situations and problems in their life.

21. To understand that there are situations and problems, and that problems are life-or-death occasions, and everything else is a situation – and situations can be handled, especially if you have a family to turn to!

Pocket Money – Should You Give It?

Summary

Pocket money is a trap that parents often fall into with the best of intentions and more generally produces less.

'A time of peace is a time when you prepare for the next conflict'. Using this principle I believe that childhood is too important to a child to waste on misleading the child. I therefore believe that as soon as possible, in all areas, a child should be prepared for the challenges and opportunities that life, and adulthood, will offer it. This does not mean that a child should have an unhappy or deprived childhood, to the contrary, I believe, and have worked hard to give my children, a rich, broad, and deep childhood based upon a true understanding of reality.

To this end I believe that pocket money should never be unconditionally given to a child but that the child should always be given the opportunity to earn pocket money. This is so that the child learns to value that which he earns, learns to relate effort with return, and values himself (or herself) as a contributing member of his family and, ultimately, society as a whole.

The amount of pocket money and the task to be done should always be clearly agreed with the child before the job is done. Initially, pocket money can be offered for very simple tasks, like replacing toys, or attempts at the child tidying his own room. Later on, specific jobs in helping around the house can be remunerated. However, the aim should be that the child, as it matures, makes an unpaid proportionate contribution to assisting in the chores of the home and that pocket money is paid for specific jobs outside of its reasonable domestic contribution.

Why Do Bad Things Happen to Good People and Good Things Happen to Bad People?

Summary

Man has always sought for a method of being on the correct side of life. Most religions are based upon the premise that, by following their rules, then benefits, or at least the avoidance of punishments, would follow in this or the next life. Adherents are often deeply disturbed by the reality that, having followed various 'divine' formulas, unpleasant events happen to them and, which often seems to offend them most, that others who have not followed the rules, prosper.

Good and bad are all often highly relative, insofar as they affect an individual. For example, the person who loses his wallet suffers, while the person who finds it benefits. An event, in itself, has to be considered in the context of the perspective of the person affected.

We continually, both consciously and sub-consciously, attempt to understand patterns in life, by relating various unrelated events so as to establish a common factor. For example, as we walk past strangers, if we notice that their eyes are all directed to a particular part of our anatomy then we search to see if our clothing is disarranged. We may recognise that often, when we go outside without an umbrella, it rains. From these events we establish rules that prevent us suffering in future, i.e. we always check our appearance in the mirror and always take an umbrella before going out. Events happen, insofar as they are predictable, and if we learn and predict them correctly we can make the best of each situation, neutralising or mitigating the bad and optimising the good.

Everything happens because of a cause. A mass murderer may win a lottery (because he bought a ticket), while a devout religious practitioner may have his child suffer a dreadful disease (because of an inherited genetic disorder). When something happens to us it has occurred because, either, we have made it happen by our actions. (We have won the Lottery because we bought a ticket) Someone else has made it happen (We won the Lottery because someone else bought and then gave us a ticket) or it was caused by actions beyond our, or anyone else's, control (We are struck by lightening).

In understanding why a good or bad consequence has occurred, we must separate from the generality of life, the sequence of events relating to that particular consequence. A person can be morally pure but economically incompetent and, in consequence, he may suffer a series of catastrophic financial events. His moral purity is not a guarantee of financial success. Similarly, financial probity is no guarantee of physical health. The question 'Why me?' is the wrong question. The correct question should be 'What must I do to guarantee what I need or want?'

The Correct Attitude

A correct attitude of mind is the most important aspect in obtaining the good and avoiding the bad in life. Such an attitude primarily leads you to:

1. Look at how best to play the hand of cards that life has dealt you.
2. Accept that life is a learning curve and that your past is to be learned from. To bring you future success you've not to waste energy upon mourning your past failures nor rely upon your past successes.
3. Accept that life has to be invested in, philosophically, academically and physically.
4. Look for patterns in life that bring both benefit and harm to you and learn to enhance or alter their causality.

Last of all, we must dispense with the purely random. Random good and bad happens to everyone, and where it is as definite as a lethal lightening strike, there is nothing that can be done about it. Although there is no 'explanation', other than being in the wrong place at the wrong time, for such events, having the correct attitude of mind can create a predisposition not to be in the wrong place at the wrong time. For example, if you want to win the Lottery you must buy a ticket and if you don't want to be struck by lightening then don't play golf in the rain!

The right attitude is one of preparation, not reaction.

Exams – How to Pass Them

Summary
Exams are part of life and should be taken seriously, however, with the proper approach they become a stepladder and not a burden.

Following our discussion last night I wanted to confirm to you my belief that if you wish to pass your examinations well then you must as a minimum:

1. Attend your lessons at school in a sensible and constructive manner. When you return home each day spend at least two hours doing the following:

    a. Complete the homework set for you that evening if possible while the subject and question is still fresh in your mind.

    b. Review each lesson and ensure that you understand what you have been taught that day. Should you be unsure on any point then either research it yourself or ask your teacher to explain it further and fully to you.

    c. Prepare for each of your lessons the next day by pre-reading each subject to ensure that you have an outline knowledge of what you will be learning.

    d. At least once a week confirm with each subject teacher that you are, in his or her opinion, up-to-date and on top of that subject. If they disagree then discuss with them a programme to bring you up-to-date.

    e. If you have any problems that you can't answer following the above programme then see me the same day so we may agree a course of action to answer the problem.

    f. On Saturday and Sunday, again review the work you have done during the week, spending at least two hours each day on this review, covering every subject, and in particular going over any areas of which you are not sure.

I trust that these rules help you and I am confident that if you follow them every week you will have a good chance of getting good marks.

The Nature of God

Summary
God is everything – everything is God.

God is not a part of the universe, God is the universe. The word God is a word we use to describe the entirety of the universe in every dimension and aspect. God is not an entity that exists within the universe, God is, literally, everything, and the universe, as we know it, exists within God.

How Do We Relate To God?

We exist within God and serve his purpose in all aspects of our life. I believe relating ourselves to the bacteria that live within our own stomachs best analogises our relationship with God. Each bacterium pursues its own existence, and aims, and in the process of doing so achieves the function it has to pursue in serving the body it is part of. Its happiness, or sadness, is irrelevant to the body. As to whether it lives a full or tortured existence is irrelevant – its will is irrelevant. The bacterium either fulfils its ideal role or not – whichever – the body's will is done.

Are We, As Individuals, Relevant – Do Our Lives Have Any Meaning?

Yes and no. First of all 'no' because what we do happens within God and God's will is inevitable. However, by understanding the true nature of God and our relationship with Him/Her this allows us to understand how life and reality works and how we best fulfil our true role. This gives our life meaning, value, satisfaction, and happiness. We can choose to work in accordance with God's plan or in a manner that avoids our true function.

What is Our True Role?

I believe that God is infinite and that the physical universe we see is his physical manifestation. I also believe that this universe is only a part of God, a little like an iceberg where one sees only the small portion of its entirety showing above the water, with the majority unseen. (I accept that this is an inaccurate analogy as God is everything and, consequently, is not floating in a sea.)

The physical manifestation of him we see is the physical universe. However, I also believe that God employs a number of mechanisms to achieve his infiniteness. In essence, I believe that God assumes his physical existence through the creation of the physical universe, which has, in the nature of physical existence, its inevitable winding-down, and its recreation. Eternity in God's physical manifestation being demonstrated in a cycle of continuous, creation ('big bang') winding-down ('entropy') and re-consolidation, leading to a repeat of this cycle.

As far as we know there are at least 1000, million, trillion stars in our galaxy and at least 1000, million, trillion galaxies in our known universe. Many of these stars have planets orbiting them and if sentient life is a naturally occurring phenomena then statistically there should be, at least, millions of civilisations active in the known universe. It would seem reasonable that such civilisations would have visited us or, at least, established some form of radio communication with us.

In the absence of verifiable evidence demonstrating such existence, it is reasonable to presume that such bodies of life do not exist, and that Man is alone and unique in the universe. If this is so then we must ask, 'Why?'

Why is it that God has chosen to have only one sentient interactive being?

Why is it that we, as human beings, have only one system of gastrointestinal bacteria?

In the second case it is because that is all that is necessary to do the job. Each individual bacterium is irrelevant as long as collectively it does its job. I believe, similarly, that God has a divine purpose for each part of his creation, even if the part is evolving to achieve its divine purpose. Its ultimate purpose may not be apparent during its evolution; however, its evolutionary path is necessary to achieve its ultimate form to achieve God's purpose.

As individuals we are unimportant, God is not at all concerned about our personal suffering or happiness, and although I believe that it may be possible to 'tap into' God's force, I do not believe that it is in the nature of reality for God to be an individual, personal, 'caring' God. Just as we are unconcerned about our individual bacterium, and only concerned about the collective function, God is of the same view to ourselves, and as long as we are pursuing God's purpose, and performing our assigned collective function, then God is satisfied.

So what about humans, what do I believe is their ultimate purpose?

I believe that the divine role of humanity is to collect, organise, understand and use information, for the purpose of completely understanding God's physical universe, with the ultimate purpose of restarting creation!

I believe that in the nature of physical reality God has designed a system, like plants produce seeds and animals reproduce, to ensure his continued eternal physical manifestation. This system accepts the decay of one state while carrying within it a mechanism to recreate it. We are that mechanism. Our function is to understand the universe and to be able to restart it at the end of its collapse.

So, what's our personal function and what's in it for us as individuals? Well, the closer we are to our assigned divine role the better our life is both as individuals and as a society. Like swimming in a river, if you swim with the flow it is far easier than attempting to swim across it or in opposition to it. Let the stream carry you, you still have to apply effort, however, your effort is far more productive, and less effort will carry you further. Life becomes far more rewarding by following God's assigned role because achievement is far easier, and rewards are more forthcoming, and readily accessible. On a personal note, we pursue God's purpose by learning a section of knowledge that we can use productively and by reproducing successfully (having children who understand and accept God's purpose). On a social note, where society's values enhance these aims for its citizens, it prospers and where it ceases to do so, it dies.

So how does one live one's everyday life? What is 'Good' and what is 'Evil'? Can God intercede in my everyday life if I appeal to him?

Everyday life is fulfilling God's aim for us. Find an area in life that appeals to you and build it into a career. Find a partner you can relate to in a meaningful manner because children, particularly when they are young, are far more stable and stronger from two ever-present parents. Have at least two children (more, if you can afford the cost and give the time but have at least two) and ensure that they understand God's design.

Praying – Should You Do it and Does it Work?

Hymie went to the Synagogue to speak to God, he said, 'God, I've always worshipped you and observed your rules and never asked for anything in return, but now I have problems that are beyond my control and I need your help. My wife spends money like there's no tomorrow, my business is having a terrible time and, in short, I'm about to be bankrupted. I need your help and I've worked out what I want you to do. I want you to make me win the Lottery – that should sort out all of my debts and make my life comfortable. I'll give you the week to sort it out and come and speak to you next Saturday.' The following Saturday Hymie returned but he was not a happy man. 'Lord, time's pressing and so are my creditors. I've told you my problem and told you the solution now please get on with it, I can't keep hanging on much longer. I'll be back next week.' The following week Hymie returned, 'Look, what sort of God do you think you are?' He demanded, 'I've told you my problems, even done your job for you and given you the answer and nothing has happened. What do you think you are doing? Suddenly, the roof opened and a beam of golden light shone on Hymie and a great voice called out in despair, 'Hymie, Hymie, Hymie, meet me half-way… buy a ticket!'

Summary

I believe that prayer is good, however, it must be done correctly, for the correct reasons and in the correct manner.

Re: What difference does Petitionary prayer make?

Dear Francis,

I would, again, start off by commenting that I find this an excellent piece of work. I'm particularly impressed by your grasp of the nature of the concept that for your prayers to have value one has to have faith without proof. Of course, how can one possibly have faith, absolute belief, in anything, without proof, unless one is deranged? It is interesting to note, at this point, that Buddhism teaches, 'Almost all religions are built on faith – rather 'blind' faith it would seem. But in Buddhism emphasis is laid on 'seeing knowing and understanding' and not on unfounded 'faith' or 'belief'. In Buddhist texts there is a word 'saddha' which is usually translated as 'faith' or 'belief' but is really 'Confidence born out of conviction (understanding) The teaching of the Buddha is qualified as "ehi-passika", that is, inviting the student to "come and see", and not "come and believe".' Walpola Rahula – What the Buddha taught' Ps.8–9.

The trick of Monotheistic churches has always been to convince their congregations that they are the only path to God and his Grace and that the congregation should accept, unquestioningly (with 'faith'), whatever they are told. Viz: 'Yesterday, the Russians were ungodly and should be destroyed. The year before it was the French. This year it's the Germans who are bad. (Never mind that last year they were our allies against the horrid French). Tomorrow it'll be the Russians or, maybe, the Iraqis. 'In the meanwhile give us (the Church) your money and you'll be rewarded in the next life/karma.' Remember Mr Orwell's 1984?

Anyhow, what's my view on 'Petitionary Prayer'? I believe in it, in the manner you've touched upon in your essay. A human's prayer will not alter the nature of God or his actions, however, by formulating a request and meditating upon it this can lead to finding the way to achieve it.

It is my belief that 'to pray' is from the Latin/Spanish verb 'pregunta' (to ask) and the process of praying, that we understand today, is a corruption of an eastern meditative process used to resolve 'situations' by allowing the intellectual digestion of the component factors of a situation into either an answer or a series of questions, which, when resolved, answer the situation.

In my experience, 'I Ching', uses this process very effectively and I have often found it to be very helpful. I have taught to you that the nature of God is that God is everything (Everything is God) and that God has a direction and purpose, which we may only guess at. I have used the analogy of the relationship of single bacteria in your stomach to you to exemplify how I understand our relationship with God. (We, individually, are even less significant within God than the bacteria within us). The aims, hopes, happiness's and sufferings of individual abdominal bacteria are irrelevant to us. Were the bacteria able to pray, their individual prayers would be as irrelevant to us, as ours are to God. I do, however, believe that in meditating upon issues and situations and evolving a 'want' either for our own best interests or to answer something we believe in, we are, in fact, seeing what we believe is the truth of what is occurring and then how best to achieve our aims. God (everything – including us) will proceed in his 'direction', which may be composed of many different 'directions' simultaneously. Our 'praying' is aimed at, firstly, seeing those relevant 'directions' correctly. Secondly, understanding how we relate to these relevant 'directions' and finally, placing ourselves, or taking actions, to use these 'directions' to give us what we want.

I always use this mantra when I'm perplexed, 'Let me see the truth. Let me understand it and let me use it' In this context the 'Truth' is the reality of the aspect of God that I am experiencing at that time. For example: I'm unhappy in my employment – do I stay or look for another job? If I decide that what I really want is more money and that it's in my best career interests to stay – then how can I increase my remuneration? If the answer to this is to achieve promotion – then how can I best achieve this? In this case it may be by improving my timekeeping, my productivity, my attitude, my appearance (to appeal to the boss' tastes not my friends) and my qualifications. Or it may be by just giving the boss one! (Joke!). By praying, I work to see what is the truth in a situation and how best to come to terms with and use it.

I have read on many occasions and believe it to be true from my own experience that when faced with a situation and unsure as to what to do then the process of dealing with the situation is as follows:

1. *Meditate upon the situation you are unsure about. That is, think about it. Establish a time by when you ideally require an answer and a time by when you must have an answer.*

2. *If no answer presents itself fairly quickly then look for more information. The process of accumulating new information is in itself a significant part of the answer because you have to decide what sort of information you must research. That, in itself, begins to define the situation.*

3. *Having accumulated all of the information reasonably available to you then you must give yourself time to digest it, (meditate) and ask your mind to give you an answer; or a further question to research.*

4. *If no answer comes to you by your ideal point, make yourself come to an answer. Although this can be wrong, usually it won't be and in most situations even a wrong answer is better than no answer. Meditate upon your answer, you still have time to change it and often having an answer polarises your situation and allows you to clarify it. However, if you don't come up with a better answer then by your must point at least you have answered your problem and have tested your answer in preparation for its use.*

I don't know if this is of any use to you but I have enjoyed both reading your essay and writing this – so send me more!

    Love,

Guru Dad

Dad, this is the first draught of an essay I started at ten o'clock this morning, it is now 15:45 and I'm about to dash into the gym then barracks. I suggest you cut and paste the essay into Word for easier reading. Again, it is the first draught so please feel free to suggest amendments if you have the time.

What difference does Petitionary prayer make?

Frank Roseman

It is natural for humans to want to pray. This leads, I believe, from Freud's concept of the 'Super Ego', that is to say that we, as children, begin life measuring our actions by the reactions of our parents, much as an animal might, gauging whether doing this or that will get him punished or rewarded. Having established this basic appreciation, then we move on to assumed (or anticipated) punishments or rewards, this eventually shows us the difference between good and bad (our initial set of moral values). As we mature, the rule against which we measure our actions becomes more complex, developing into a combination of an ideal person (he whom we aspire to imitate – perhaps a parent figure or a manufactured self image – the Super Ego effectively), and the concept of a greater being; one who would be constantly watching over us – an extended parental role – fulfilled for us by a god.

Whilst for the majority of the time most of us would dismiss this idea out of hand, come a time of crisis, or severe testing, these same people will more often than not, turn to whatever image of God they hold and ask him for help. There is a military maxim that goes, 'There is no such thing as an atheist in a foxhole', which illustrates my point. It is this form of prayer that we call petitionary prayer – prayer that asks God for something. The petitioner seeks by every indication and argument to move God to fulfil his wish.

Our subject matter now established, the first point to be tackled is, logically: does it work? In Mathew 21:22 Jesus said to his disciples 'Whatever you pray for in faith you will receive'. Now his use of the word faith there will prove to be somewhat important. Beforehand, however, the conflict between Elijah and the prophets of Baal, as described in Kings 18, strikes an interesting note: 'Elijah's opponents believed that the God Baal answered prayers and on the basis of this belief they called on Baal all day long – but to no avail. Thus their belief in the efficacy of their prayers was falsified. Elijah believed that Yahweh was God and he would answer the prayers of those who called on him. On the basis of this belief he prayed to Yahweh who answered his prayer by sending fire from heaven. Thus his belief in the God of Abraham was confirmed before the assembled multitude on Mount Carmel.' Elijah was sufficiently confident that his God (Yahweh) would act in direct answer to his prayers, that he stood atop a mountain and demonstrated it. Though this worked in the story, there are problems inherent in testing God. The first of these is the question of whether we can carry out tests on the efficacy of prayer without being seen as irreligious or blasphemous because are we not 'forbidden to put the Lord to test' (Mathew 4:7)? Assuming that we can negotiate our way around this small hurdle, we then find ourselves confronted by a much more substantial one: part of the words quoted from Jesus earlier on is, that faith like that of Elijah is a necessary condition for prayers to be granted. This implies that an experiment to test the efficacy must necessarily be a self-defeating exercise, as, in order to view the prayer as valid material to be experimented upon, one would have to have some form of doubt in it in the first place. That is to say that as in testing a scientific theory, a belief is held with no more than tentative adherence (lest it be falsified) as in each test there is a risk, this analytical attitude excludes the kind of faith which is necessary for prayer to be efficacious. In order to examine something and prove it to be a scientific (-esque) theory, from whence predictions may be derived, such that is either confirmed or falsified by certain results, one would conduct an experiment, well illustrated by Einstein's theory of gravitation, described by Karl Popper as follows: 'Einstein's gravitational theory had lead to the result that light must be attracted by heavy bodies (such as the sun), precisely as material bodies were attracted. As a consequence it could be calculated that light from a distant star, whose apparent position was close to the sun, would reach the earth from such a direction that the star would seem to be slightly shifted away from the sun;

or, in other words, that stars close to the sun would look as if they had moved a little away from the sun and from one another. This is a thing, which cannot normally be observed since the sun's overwhelming brightness renders such stars invisible during daytime; but during an eclipse it is possible to take photographs of them. If the same constellation is photographed at night, one can measure the distance on the two photographs, and check the effect.' Now, the advantage of Einstein's theory was that it was genuinely scientific, that is to say that it could be repeated, and, provided it was true, then the results could be consistently predicted as such physical objects are bound by causal necessity. Unfortunately a request (a prayer) is not by itself a sufficient causal condition making it inevitable that the person to whom the request is addressed does what is requested. Impersonal objects like machines, however, can be manipulated as they are governed by causal necessity, I only have to arrange the correct causal conditions (e.g. pulling the relevant leaver) and the desired effects follow inevitably. Sentient beings (a category within which I shall place God, admittedly a dangerous supposition, but for the sake of the argument, it will suffice) cannot be manipulated in this way. Because someone's decision to act cannot be made inevitable, he can be coaxed, bribed or persuaded but not bound inevitably.

We can argue, then, that an attempt to test the efficacy of prayer through scientific experiment assumes that prayer is a manipulative technique and that God, rather than being a sentient being, is somewhat closer to a machine. It then must put the relationship between God and man at an impersonal manipulative level as opposed to a person alone. Lest we now go off at too much of a tangent, coming back to the question: we are not, as yet, entirely sure as to whether petitionary prayer makes any direct difference to the circumstances of the petitioner. As it stands, our examination of the method by logical means does not make it appear altogether probable. Therefore, let us now move on and examine the potential results as opposed to the method.

If I cannot examine my prayers and their results without fear of rendering them sterile through lack of faith, perhaps as an outside agent I could investigate the probability of requests being granted in a way that could be shown statistically, thus avoiding the difficulties involved in an experimental test.

Sir Frances Galton carried out just such an investigation in 1883. Does public prayer have any real effect on, for example, longevity? he asked. He investigated the lives of those who are most often prayed for – in this case the sovereign of every state ('Grant her in health long to live' and other such variations) and found that the mean age of males of various classes of those who had survived their thirtieth year, during the years of 1758 to 1843, the sovereigns were by far the shortest lived of them all. This would suggest that the public prayer, therefore, had no effect. The only counter argument is that the conditions of royal life may be naturally more fatal, thus resulting in less timely deaths despite the public prayer.

A similar example, a part of the same investigation, was that of the longevity of the clergy. When compared to lawyers and doctors, they are found to live not a great deal longer, which is surprising if one were to remember that 'it is their profession to pray, and they have the practice of offering morning and evening family prayers in addition to their public devotions.' Men of the clergy are surely to be assumed to be more worthy of God's love and appreciation, yet their prayers for 'protection against the perils and dangers of the night, for security during the day, and from recovery from sickness, appear to be futile in the result.'

The last example Galton gives is a financial one. He suggests that 'if prayerful habits had influence on temporal success, it is very probable that insurance offices, of at least some descriptions would have long ago have discovered and made allowance for it.' This seems not to have happened, as apparently even 'Quakers, who are most devout and most shrewd men of business, have ignored these considerations.' So why would they do this if it is not simply that 'they do not really believe in what they and others freely assert about the efficacy of prayer'?

Galton concluded that 'many items of ancient faith have been successively abandoned by the Christian world to the domains of recognised superstition' something he feels should happen to 'the belief in the efficacy of prayer' he feels that in the 'sense in which [he] has been considering it, must be yielded also.' A response was later put forward that Galton based his statistical enquiry on too small a group to make it a fair investigation, but I would argue that surely this can have no relevance as God, in his omnipotence should be able to give equal treatment to all people at all times, and as a man may die only once, it must be as important to him that individuals are looked after (i.e. him) as opposed to the mean. Overall, however, I feel that Galton did the pursuit of truth in this area a good service in showing from another angle that direct results from petitionary prayer were not to be depended on.

Perhaps then, a slightly different angle should be taken in looking for an answer. Aquinas narrowly avoided such an answer in his solution to a problem for petitionary prayer put forward by Calvin, with a little adjustment, I should think he would have had it. Calvin argued thus: 'Some one will say, Does he not know, both what our difficulties are, and what is meet for our interest, so that it seems in some measure superfluous to solicit him by our prayers, as if he were winking, or even sleeping, until roused by the sound of our voice?' And Aquinas answered thus: 'We must pray, not in order to inform God of our needs and desires, but in order to remind ourselves that in these matters we need divine assistance.'

I believe that whilst petitionary prayer may not invoke God to act directly in answer (in the way that was used to satisfy Elijah's critics on Mount Carmel) it does still serve a purpose within us. That is to say that, as Ceslaus Veleck claimed; ' in so far as prayer affects anything at all, it affects ourselves, not God. We do not pray to sway God. We pray in order to change and to dispose ourselves so as to receive properly what God has willed to give us.' What it is that God has 'willed to give us' is again arguable and is a concept with which I would not entirely agree, but he went on to suggest that 'through this change in attitude, the person who prays becomes better able to cope with the way things go in the world. In this way one might experience, through prayer, an increase of spiritual strength or grace in the face of adversity, something I feel is as close to an answer as I have seen yet. Now conclude, again with a comment from Calvin: 'Although God complies with a request, he does not always give an answer in the very terms of our prayer, but while apparently holding us in suspense, yet in an unknown way, shows that our prayers have not been in vain.' That is to say that when dealing with a personal God, who is also said to be omnipotent, omniscient and omnipresent, to him 'all hearts are open, all desires are known'. God, whose agenda is (hypothetically) far beyond our human comprehension, may chose to answer prayer not in direct, physical action, but instead by having us use prayer to compose our minds and thoughts, such that we can answer our own problems. This, I believe is the difference that petitionary prayer makes.

Can You Trust Them – Accountants, Lawyers And The Government?

Sed quis custodiet ipsos custodes – Who supervises the supervisors?'

(Juvenal, Satires)

The World's three most often told lies:
1. 'Sorry, Officer, I didn't realise I was driving at over thirty miles per hour.'
2. 'There's a cheque in the post.'
3. 'I'm from the Government and here to help you.'

Summary
Accountants, lawyers, and the Government are like fire, very dangerous if handled or used without great caution. The correct attitude to them all is to treat each one as vicious predators who are looking to exploit every vulnerability you expose.

Why use accountants or lawyers and, surely, the Government is, 'of the People, for the People, by the People'?

In 1913, when Britain controlled roughly, 30% of the world's surface and 28% of the world's population Britain spent only 4% of its gross national product on running the whole of the Empire. This was at a time when the British working man probably had the highest standard of living in the world! Today, the British Government admits to around 40% of GDP! (My calculations show it to be well in excess of 50%.) The French Government admits to 54% – the shape of the future for Britain! Before the age of computers, when all documentation had to be kept by manual records, fewer people were employed in administering the whole of the Empire than are employed today, in just two of the departments of the British bureaucracy, the present British Inland Revenue and Customs and Excise.

It is frightening to realise that the enormous process of

'nationalisation', which in Britain, in the 1950s, led to the State ownership of just about all of the great economic engines that had produced Britain's prosperity for the previous two hundred years – coal mining, iron and steel production, railways, shipbuilding, the aircraft industry, the telephone industry and, of course, education and the health industry, as well as, latterly, the car industry. This process of State ownership, without exception, ended up in disaster and the virtual extinction of these industries along with the destruction of millions of people's lives and large sections of the Nation. As with the USSR, it was resoundingly demonstrated that the Government could not administer the production of any product or service successfully. 'Nationalisation' along with the inevitable consequent growth of Government bureaucracy, and the reversal of focus from producing a good, or service, to serve the market and the people in it, to the focus of running an industry to employ Government supporters, was the undoubted cause of the destruction of Britain as a world power and as a creator of wealth and prosperity for the British people.

Today's world is extremely, and to a very large extent unnecessarily, bureaucratic. However, this is a deliberate construction by nearly all governments because of the nature of modern governments. The majority of citizens in most nations are more than capable of looking after themselves within a framework that only supplies what is truly required, namely, the defence of their country and the policing of their country to maintain their physical person, personal property, commercial transactions and freedom of communications. These citizens are more than capable of arranging for other services, such as medical and educational services and they would be able to do so at a far lower cost for a far higher level of service through private insurance.

Government, as we know it today, does not want this. It does not want this because it is largely composed of vast bureaucracies that need to justify their existences by providing services that are believed to be 'needed'; they are not. Like the story of, 'The King's New Clothes', if enough people can be persuaded to believe that something exists then they will pretend to see it.

The provision of these artificially 'needed' services allows the bureaucracies to accumulate unto themselves vast powers and controls over the citizens within these countries. Because of the need of bureaucracies to justify their own existence, to maintain the incomes and benefits of the senior bureaucrats, that sit at the head of them, and the fact that through the so-called 'democratic system' the majority of the marginal voters believe that they benefit from the existence of these bureaucracies, then a system of government has developed which, parasitically, exploits the work of the wealth-creating sector of the country.

Government, today, is concerned with satisfying the wants of these bureaucracies. The main job of the Government is to extract as much wealth and power from the wealth-creators (the workers and private business people) as possible. Ministers occupy the role of 'fall-guys' who can be sacrificed to public opinion if a mistake is seen by the public. The political party that achieves power is the party that has the most to offer the bureaucracies and those sectors of society who see themselves as benefiting from the expansion of the bureaucracies, namely, accountants and lawyers.

It is demonstratively true that it is far harder to create wealth than to spend wealth. It is the policy of the Government to expand the disruptive and under-educated 'underclass' so as to justify the existence of a 'care culture' and the consequent theft of wealth from the wealth-creators. This allows a large section of the wealth created to be stolen from those who create it, and spent by those less capable than the creators. The bureaucrats largely take this expenditure with only a very small proportion being used to alleviate the 'need'. In fact, from the bureaucracy's point of view, it must not alleviate the need, as it then would have no justification to continue its own existence!

The problem with this form of system is that it is self-destroying. It must, ultimately, create conditions that destroy its foundation; the wealth-creators and the wealth-creation process.

In dealing with Government bureaucracies it is desirable to do so through the agency of a licensed professional. These professionals are agents of Government, acting in the interests of Government but paid for by you. Only by using accountants and lawyers can you have an element of protection from the whims of bureaucrats who can use almost limitless resources to oppress and exploit you. As a general principle it is best never to fight with bureaucrats on your own account but to, ideally, have your interests advocated by a professional representing a trading group. Bureaucrats are afraid of adverse publicity and are very sensitive to media exposure as large interest groups can represent voting swings. An example of the efficiency of a loosely organised, but highly effective voting group, is the homosexual lobby which has rewritten the morality of Britain and been very effective in severely damaging family life and values. Representing roughly 2% of the population they have altered life and its values for all.

Accountants

Three men are walking down a country road; one is a farmer, one an aspiring entrepreneur and the last an accountant. They find an old lamp, half-buried by the side of the road, which they excavate, and then each, in turn, give a polish. A Genie appears who says, 'Normally I give three wishes to the finder of this lamp, however, as all three of you have found and rubbed the lamp I'm giving one wish to each.' The Farmer said, 'Well as I am a Farmer and an Englishman and I love the countryside and believe that a man's home is his castle. I wish to have a lovely country house.' No sooner had he said this than he was instantly transported into a beautiful country house in the centre of a lovely country estate in the middle of England! The Entrepreneur then told the Genie, 'I've always wanted to be rich and successful. I would like £5,000,000 in cash please.' The Genie, replied, 'No problem,' then snapped his fingers and the Entrepreneur found his arms filled with £50.00 notes. He began to walk away. The Genie then turned to the accountant and asked him what he would like. The accountant thought for a moment and then said, 'I'd like 500 false share certificates and then 20 minutes with the Entrepreneur!'

Accountants have one boss, and that is the Inland Revenue. You are only one of their, maybe, one hundred clients. Should their neglect, bad advice, or incompetence lead to your bankruptcy, or destruction (commercial and/or physical), then they have ninety-nine other clients to maintain the majority of their income. The time they spent on you will now be spent in replacing you with another punter to replace the income stream you supplied. Providing their advice does not destroy all of their clients simultaneously they have a secure business – so long as they don't fall foul of the Inland Revenue.

An accountant who puts the best interests of his client before those of the Inland Revenue, and this becomes known to the Inland Revenue, will find himself branded a 'centre of infection' by the Revenue. This will mean that his life, and that of his client's, is made miserable by pedantic harassment on every aspect of dealings with the Revenue. This harassment will occur where the accountant is considered to no longer have the best interests of the Revenue firmly in mind in dealing with his clients. Where the accountant actually bends or breaks the rules, then the Revenue will gleefully prosecute and destroy him, and any offending clients. The Revenue, joyfully, using the accountant against the client and the client against the accountant.

In dealing with an accountant, the accountant will often give the client the impression that the accountant is 'bending the rules', he very rarely is. He is usually only giving this impression to lever-up his fees and/or the client's dependency on him. What the accountant may also do is to tacitly encourage the client doing the wrong thing as far as the Revenue is concerned. He may also, by failing to educate the client to the longer-term consequences of the client's actions, allow the client to carry out a course of actions that lead to later conflict with the Revenue. He will do this in a manner that will ensure that later no fault or blame can be attached to himself. He will do this so as to be able to charge the client for extracting him from the created problem. Large fees, at a premium because of, 'confidentiality', 'urgency' and 'importance' can be charged for this type of work.

Lawyers

A solicitor opened his eyes and expected to wake up in his bedroom but, instead, found himself outside of the gates to Heaven. He approached the Angel on duty at the Pearly Gates and demanded to see St. Peter. 'Why am I here?' he demanded to know. 'A mistake has been made, I've been called too early, why I'm only just beginning in life. I'm young, in excellent health, have a newly established successful practice, a beautiful young Wife and two lovely young children. I demand that you check your records!' St. Peter agreed to check and came back after 5 minutes. 'There's no mistake', he said, 'I've checked, and according to the time you have charged your clients you're 97 years old!'

Lawyers are in a similar situation, again you are one of several dozen punters and they are 'officers of the court'. Your position is less vulnerable than with an accountant as lawyers are somewhat obliged to be seen to act in your best interests and therefore have less latitude to deceive you. A useful saying I have found when dealing with lawyers is, 'You go into a lawyer with a situation and come out with a problem'. This is because a lawyer primarily sees you as a source of revenue and will mainly look at the best way to relieve you of your wealth while not, himself, breaking the law. If you take to him a situation that you do not know how to resolve, his approach will be to mould this situation into something far worse. Why does he do this? Because if he deals with your problem quickly and easily, as he would were it his own situation, he can only charge you a small fee, whereas if he either (or both) manipulates the situation, or your understanding of it, into something far worse than it is, he can charge you far more.

Why use professionals? Because you have to. The system is constructed so that even a well-educated layman can't find his way through it for most issues. A professional is necessary to deal with the bureaucracy and he knows it. He knows that you need him and he will do all that he can to extract as much for himself from the situation as possible. You can't avoid using professionals but you can use them cautiously, and remember – your need is their income and profit, so the greater they can convince you that your problem is then the more they can charge you.

Government, lawyers and accountants have common medium-term interest in having a complicated, bureaucratic system. This creates work, employment, and gives them unearned importance. They collaborate in the construction of labyrinthine structures that necessitates the use of paid-for professionals so that a business can function. It's a game – and one that exploits the capable, hard-working wealth-creators. In the long-term this approach kills industries, however, these collaborators are not concerned with the long-term, the future is the responsibility of someone else. Like the froth on the top of a glass of Guinness, even as the Guinness is drank the froth still floats on the top until there is nothing left to drink!

All empires die by being either invaded by a superior military force or, more normally, by being destroyed from within by the cancer of the corruption of its administration. Britain owned the biggest empire the world has ever seen. Never really defeated militarily, it died because of the cancer of the growth of its bureaucracy. With the bureaucracy taking more and more of the wealth of the nation and using this very wealth to destroy the nation's own ability to succeed and survive.

In dealing with accountants and lawyers, I recommend that before retaining one, you speak to at least three on the subject first, and then choose a different one using the insight gained discussing your situation with the first three. This may involve you in several other meetings until you find one you feel has the best grasp of your view on the problem, however, it is a sensible investment and can save you being unreasonably exploited. Ask for meetings on the basis, 'That you wish to discuss the possibility of them acting for you on a matter of ....' This way you will avoid having to pay for the initial meetings, can asses each person and his approach and may even find out enough information to resolve your situation without having to give instructions.

If you decide to use a professional it is vital that you agree in detail what you are trying to achieve and the associated fees with, if possible, a maximum for the matter. Remember, the lawyer or accountant views you, primarily, as a source of income and will do as little as possible to obtain as much as he can.

Information is a little like the distance of a winning racehorse in a tightly-run race. You don't need much more than your opponent, as just a little more can clinch the race. A professional may not know much more than you, however, he will know how to handle the paperwork and the bureaucracy, and if he has even a small amount more knowledge than you, he can easily make the process quite threatening and obscure. You need to neutralise this advantage as much as possible, so when dealing with small situations read around them as much as possible. Look for and ask for precedents. Look for an ombudsman, as sometimes the threat of having to deal with an ombudsman is enough to make your opponent more reasonable.

On major matters, such as substantial litigation, divorces and major criminal matters, it is best, if it can be organised, to have a lawyer advise you on how to deal with your lawyer and an accountant advise you on how to handle your accountant. This is to stop you being fed materially incorrect information that can exacerbate the situation. Having the insight from the advisory professional should, normally, lead to much smaller total fees, even though you are paying two people to do one person's job.

A technique for obtaining such an audit on a professional's work while it is in progress is to ask another professional to look at your own file of papers, saying that you are unsure as to whether a proper job is being done and that you may wish to move the work to him. It is unlikely but you may have to pay him to do this, however, you will obtain valuable insight and he should pick up any material errors. You will not be obliged to move the work and in any event the charge for the review will not be excessive, as it should take no more than an hour.

The Cradle-to-the-Grave Welfare System

Two men are sitting on a train and as the train proceeds through the countryside one of them repeatedly keeps ripping strips from his newspaper and throwing them out of the window. After an hour the other man can restrain his curiosity no longer, 'Why do you keep doing that?' he asks the newspaper tearer. 'To keep the crocodiles away,' is the reply. 'But this is England, we don't have crocodiles in England?' he responds. 'Effective, isn't it?' the newspaper tearer replies triumphantly!

An Honest Taxation System

Summary

Has it ever struck you how strange our society is? Do you ever find yourself asking why our social system seems to be determined to punish those who do the 'right thing', those who do the things that society needs them to do? Society appears determined to punish success, to punish those upon whom it depends.

For a society to survive and prosper a society, needs, and should want, its members to work productively and profitably. (No society would, sensibly, want its members to work unproductively and unprofitably, surely?) Therefore, by definition, moral good within a society is that which encourages the survival and prosperity of that society and its members.

Therefore, the moral measure of a society is how well it encourages and supports its members to do the thing which it needs for its own survival and prosperity.

Net income, is the way in which productivity is measured and, therefore, any system within a society that discourages the production of 'benevolent' income, that is, income which is derived from activities that benefit the survival and prosperity of that society is, by definition, immoral.

Income, once earned, can only be employed in just one of two ways. Spent or saved. Firstly, by saving it this is morally 'good' because by saving morally good income, the citizen contributes to the pool of capital that is available for the development of his (or her) society. Secondly, income can be spent. Income may be spent in only one of two ways; the first is upon morally good expenditure (the housing, clothing, feeding, education and enlightenment of his family) or morally bad expenditure (drugs, alcohol, cigarettes, junk food etc.).

Any society that pursues policies that contradicts its own best interests is, again, by definition, immoral, as are the policies that it pursues. Therefore, we can conclude that any tax upon income is immoral. Indiscriminate expenditure taxes are immoral, as are all capital taxes.

The obvious question asked at this point is 'How then does a society produce income to pay for itself?' The answer to this question is that a society would raise tax revenue from expenditure upon 'immoral' expenditure and, if required, by specific impost. For example a road fund tax which would actually be spent upon the designated expenditure, the maintenance and improvement of the road system, and not absorbed into the general state income as has happened in Britain. It is expected, however, that by providing an honest system a state would provide a more honest, more capable and more self-reliant people with far less justification for Government services.

An interesting aspect of the way in which society is run at present is that the process of earning money is generally considered to take more ability than spending it. Yet the nature of our present system says that the section of society that has the ability of earning does not have the ability to spend that which it produces, and consequently society has developed a panoply of mechanisms to remove the major proportion of discretionary income from high earners, and some not so discretionary income from none high earners!

We have allowed a system to grow which is destroying our future. We have created a system which not only is refusing to protect our person, our family, or our property, but which also is actively destroying the future for our children.

Putting the tax system into context we can look at the effect upon our society's policies upon its own future. It would seem reasonable to expect a society to look to encourage the more capable and better educated to reproduce while discouraging the less capable.

As it has also been repeatedly demonstrated, that the most productive and most stable members of society are from conventional two-parent, married, heterosexual households, and that most disruptive children, and consequently disruptive, criminal adults, are the products of one-parent households, it would seem reasonable to expect that our society would have worked to improve and strengthen the incentives and supports for married heterosexual unions. This has not been the case and in fact the approach of Government has been wherever possible to undermine or destroy the married state.

It is fact, established through substantial repeated research, that not only is the married state conducive to the production of children who become good members of society but that also the married state is the most conducive to the health and happiness of the couples who marry. The state, the children, and the partners all benefit. The product of present policies benefits no one other than a small, misguided but very dangerous, group in the short to medium term.

In a world where the need for a society is to have educated and productive citizens, laws and motivations that deter the establishment, and maintenance of stable unions between heterosexual couples, and the production by them, of stable children, is obviously contrary to the best interests of the state, its citizens and their children. Capable and educated adults should be motivated and rewarded for having stable children. Society needs to invest in its future and the best initial investment is to stop punishing the very people and systems that society needs to work for it.

We have dying birth rates among our most capable people because our society treats them as an exploitable commodity, which will continue to produce irrespective of what is done to them. While the reality is that this is not the case, our more capable citizens are choosing marriage much less. They are choosing to have fewer children; they see a state that gives lip-service to the idea of marriage and children but that treats the capable, educated family, as an easily exploitable tax source, too overworked meeting its family and tax obligations, and too committed to its physical location to be able to actively defend itself.

The introduction of 'Cottaging' laws, ostensibly to 'protect the rights of a minority' effectively does serious damage to freedoms of the majority. The reality will be that public toilets will become the hunting ground of predatorial homosexuals and the rights of the majority will become seriously damaged. Our children will be the most vulnerable. Who will ever feel comfortable allowing their child to use a public toilet in future?

Our society is separated into two groups, those in public employment and those in the wealth creation sector.

The public sector continues to grow, consuming an ever-increasing section of the national wealth while producing no wealth itself. Its power springs from the fact that it usually occupies a monopoly position within society and that this monopoly position is protected by its control of the Government. It can dictate its terms and conditions of employment and is able, generally, to avoid any responsibility for the consequences of its abuses of power or failure to carry out its responsibilities. For example, all nationalised industries have failed and the failure of the various public services, from the NHS to those departments charged with protecting children, is beyond dispute. The British police service is increasingly seen as self-serving, dishonest, and incompetent, as is the national fire service, whose recent, very successful 'cover', by a partially-trained force numbering 35% of the FBS with 50-year-old equipment, demonstrated how over-manned and underemployed they are.

The wealth-creating sector – the 'private sector' – is treated by Government as a source of wealth which will produce without care or consideration. This sector continues to shrink, particularly the real wealth-producing foundation, the manufacturing section. Crushed by taxes, an artificially high exchange rate, relatively high interests rates, ludicrous employment laws, regulatory burdens and bureaucratic intervention. The many new Government-sponsored bureaucracies have obscured its demise. These create employment although they consume, not produce, wealth. The headline rates of employment do not reveal that the employees in the wealth-creating sectors, being thrown out of work, are not the same people being employed by the new bureaucracies. (Very few Government departments have employment for welders, machinists, engineers, or technicians). The new bureaucracies absorb educated people, who would otherwise have found employment within industry or commerce, and gives them a 'career' in processing paper. We are destroying our seed-corn for tomorrow.

The wealth-creating sector is used as a mechanism of social change, a tax collection mechanism, and a source of tax revenue. It is also used to handle the real challenges wherever they are found within the public sector. For example, the security attendants at employment offices are from private companies as are the consultants who advise the civil servants on any issue that requires competence or may be in any way contentious.

One further area of concern is the way in which, in a similar situation to the Church, in medieval England and Europe, that the treatment of breaches of the law by civil servants, like the medieval clergy, is not given the same treatment as breaches by normal citizens. The abuse and death of a child supervised by a social worker results in that civil servant being possibly dismissed with a derisory penalty and then awarded £50,000 compensation! Had the same offence occurred in the private sector the responsible employee could well have faced a prosecution for manslaughter.

The construction of an underclass appears to be the undeclared aim of the Government. The creation of a substantial section of the population that is uneducated, culturally deprived, and disruptive, is evidenced by Government policies on education, policing and immigration as well as the Government's approach to families, taxation and social priorities. Why is this? If we follow the logic that 'If it looks like a duck, quacks like a duck and acts like a duck then it probably is a duck' then we can deduce from the Government's actions that this policy is deliberate and has a purpose. The purpose of the creation of this underclass is to justify the continuation and expansion of the majority of the bureaucracy of Britain.

The only services the state really needs to provide for its citizens are: defence of the nation from outside attack, and defence of the persons, family, and property of the citizens, within the state, through an efficient proactive police force. Health, education, insurance, pensions, and associated services, can be easily, more efficiently, and far less expensively, provided by legislation and private mechanisms than by the state. The Government could still legislate for minimums and obligations of levels of service leaving private enterprise to compete to provide the actual services. Left to themselves the majority of the natural population of Britain (including second generation immigrants) could provide for themselves quite adequately within the two state provided services.

The Government is very aware of this reality, however, it also realises that should it accept this reality, while this would empower the nation and its citizens, it would be reducing itself to a peripheral role in the operation of the nation. Its deliberate policy is to create an uneducated (even miseducated) disruptive underclass, so as to justify its continuation as the needed provider of social services and its consequent confiscation (legal theft) of wealth. This allows the Government to justify taking large amounts of wealth from the wealth-creators (who are busy working) to answer social problems which it has, by its own policies, created.

Capital is someone's unspent income; profit is a measure of relative efficiency.

Slavery, communism, and socialism are political systems (excuses for theft) within which the person who earns wealth has the wealth he has created taken from him and spent by someone else, normally a bureaucrat of some type.

Capitalism is a system where the person who earns wealth may decide on how it will be spent. Capitalism places responsibility in the hands of those people who have the power – it's a balanced system.

Bureaucrats normally believe in a system where they should be able to choose how to spend their own money while also believing that they should deny that same freedom to wealth-creators!

'You are cleverer than I, insofar as you are able to create wealth, while I am not, however, you are not as clever as I in deciding how to spend the wealth that you have created!' seems to summarise the attitude of state bureaucrats.

Bibliography

HEALTH:

Campbell, Giraud W, *A Doctor's Proven New Home Cure for Arthritis*
Diamond, Harvey, *Fit for Life*

WEALTH:

Leboeuf, Michael, *How to Motivate People*
Markert, Christopher, *I Ching*
Kiyosaki, Robert, *Rich Dad, Poor Dad*
McCormack, Mark H, *The Terrible Truth About Lawyers*

REALITY:

Orwell, George, *1984*
Coxall, B, and L Robins, *Contemporary British Politics* (Edited yearly)
Rogers, Jim, *Investment Biker & Adventure Capitalist*
Buchanan, Patrick, *The Death of the West*
Peter, Laurence J, *The Peter Pyramid*
Wardner, James W, *The Planned Destruction of America*
Crichton, Michael, *The Rising Sun*
Kaplan, Robert, *Warrior Politics*

PHILOSOPHY:

Various, *The Art of War*
Popkin, RHP, and A Stroll, *Philosophy Made Simple*
Rahula, Walpola, *What the Buddha Taught*
Machiavelli, *The Prince*

Lifestyle Factors:

Unhealthy lifestyle choices significantly increase the risk of Type 2 diabetes. Poor dietary habits, lack of physical activity, and obesity contribute to insulin resistance and impaired glucose metabolism. Addressing these lifestyle factors through healthy eating, regular exercise, and weight management is essential for diabetes prevention and management.

Age and Ethnicity:

Age is a non-modifiable risk factor for diabetes, with the risk increasing with age. Additionally, certain ethnic groups, including African Americans, Hispanic/Latino Americans, Native Americans, and Asian Americans, are more prone to developing diabetes. Understanding these demographic risk factors allows for targeted interventions and screenings.

Gestational Diabetes Risk Factors:

For gestational diabetes, risk factors include being overweight, having a family history of diabetes, and being older than 25 during pregnancy. Identifying these risk factors early in pregnancy enables proactive monitoring and management to prevent complications.

Understanding the causes and risk factors of diabetes facilitates a proactive approach to prevention and management. By addressing modifiable risk factors through lifestyle modifications and monitoring non-modifiable factors, individuals can take charge of their health and reduce the likelihood of developing diabetes.

2.3 Symptoms and Diagnosis

Recognizing the symptoms of diabetes is crucial for early diagnosis and intervention. While the symptoms may vary between Type 1 and Type 2 diabetes, understanding the common signs allows individuals and healthcare professionals to initiate timely assessments.

Common Symptoms:

- **Frequent Urination:** Excess sugar in the blood leads to increased urine production, causing frequent trips to the bathroom.

- **Excessive Thirst:** Dehydration from frequent urination triggers an intense thirst as the body attempts to replenish lost fluids.

- **Unexplained Weight Loss:** In Type 1 diabetes, the body may break down muscle and fat for energy, resulting in weight loss despite increased appetite.

- **Increased Hunger:** The lack of insulin's effectiveness in Type 2 diabetes can lead to a feeling of constant hunger.

- **Fatigue:** The body's inability to effectively use glucose for energy can result in persistent fatigue and weakness.

Symptoms Specific to Type 1 and Type 2:

- **Type 1 Diabetes:** Rapid onset of symptoms, including extreme thirst, frequent urination, and unexplained weight loss. Symptoms may progress quickly, leading to a diabetic emergency if left untreated.

- **Type 2 Diabetes:** Symptoms may develop gradually and can include blurred vision, slow healing of wounds, and recurring infections.

Diagnostic Methods:

Diagnosing diabetes involves various tests to assess blood sugar levels and overall glucose metabolism. Common diagnostic tests include:

- **Fasting Blood Sugar Test:** Measures blood sugar levels after an overnight fast.

- **Oral Glucose Tolerance Test (OGTT):** Involves fasting overnight and then drinking a sugary solution, with blood sugar levels measured at intervals.

- **Hemoglobin A1c Test:** Provides an average of blood sugar levels over the past two to three months.

Understanding the symptoms and diagnostic methods allows individuals to seek medical attention promptly. Early diagnosis is crucial for initiating appropriate treatment and preventing complications associated with uncontrolled diabetes.

2.4 Blood Sugar Monitoring

Blood sugar monitoring is a cornerstone of diabetes management, empowering individuals to make informed decisions about their health. This process involves regular testing to assess blood glucose levels and adjusting lifestyle factors and medication accordingly.

Monitoring Methods:

- **Self-monitoring of Blood Glucose (SMBG):** Involves using a glucose meter to measure blood sugar levels at home. Regular monitoring provides insights into how food, physical activity, and medication affect blood sugar.

- **Continuous Glucose Monitoring (CGM):** A wearable device that continuously tracks blood sugar levels throughout the day. CGM systems provide real-time data and trends, offering a comprehensive view of glucose fluctuations.

Target Ranges:

Understanding target blood sugar ranges is crucial for effective management. The American Diabetes Association recommends the following general targets:

- **Fasting Blood Sugar:** 80-130 mg/dL before meals.

- **Postprandial (After Meals):** Below 180 mg/dL.

Individualized targets may vary based on factors such as age, overall health, and the presence of complications.

Interpreting Results:

Regular monitoring allows individuals to interpret their blood sugar readings and take appropriate actions. Consistently high or low readings may indicate the need for adjustments in diet, medication, or physical activity. Trends observed over time provide valuable information for refining diabetes management strategies.

Integration into Daily Life:

Blood sugar monitoring becomes a routine aspect of daily life for individuals with diabetes. It involves understanding the impact of various factors, such as food choices and exercise, on blood sugar levels. The information gleaned from monitoring helps individuals make proactive decisions to maintain optimal blood sugar control.

Technology and Innovation:

Advancements in technology have transformed blood sugar monitoring. Continuous Glucose Monitoring (CGM) systems, smartphone apps, and integrated healthcare platforms streamline the monitoring process. These innovations not only enhance accuracy but also promote greater convenience and accessibility.

Blood sugar monitoring is a dynamic and empowering aspect of diabetes management. By understanding the methods, target ranges, and interpretation of results, individuals can actively participate in their healthcare journey. Regular monitoring serves as a compass, guiding individuals toward optimal blood sugar control and overall well-being.

Endomorph Body Type

3.1 Characteristics of an Endomorph

Understanding the characteristics of an endomorph body type lays the groundwork for effective health management, especially when dealing with conditions like diabetes. Endomorphs typically exhibit specific physical traits that distinguish them from other body types, such as ectomorphs and mesomorphs.

Body Composition:

The primary characteristic of an endomorph is a higher percentage of body fat. Endomorphs tend to store excess calories as fat, and their bodies may have a rounder or softer appearance. This distribution of body fat is often concentrated around the abdomen, hips, and thighs.

Slower Metabolism:

Endomorphs often experience a slower metabolism compared to other body types. A slower metabolism means the body burns calories at a slower rate, making it easier for endomorphs to gain weight, particularly when consuming excess calories. This metabolic trait can pose challenges when it comes to weight management and requires a tailored approach to diet and exercise.

Muscle Mass:

While endomorphs may have a higher percentage of body fat, they also possess a natural predisposition to carry more muscle mass. This can be advantageous in certain aspects of fitness and exercise, as muscle mass plays a role in metabolic rate and overall strength.

Resistance to Weight Loss:

Endomorphs may find it more challenging to lose weight compared to other body types. The body's natural tendency to store fat can make it difficult to achieve and maintain a lower body weight. This resistance to weight loss requires a comprehensive and sustainable approach to diet and physical activity.

Bone Structure:

Endomorphs typically have a wider bone structure, contributing to their sturdier and more robust appearance. While this can be advantageous for activities that require strength, it also means that excess weight can be distributed more prominently, emphasizing the need for proactive weight management.

Understanding these physical characteristics allows individuals to embrace their unique body types and tailor their approach to health and fitness accordingly. Rather than viewing these traits as limitations, recognizing the strengths of an endomorph body type empowers individuals to make informed decisions for overall well-being.

3.2 Metabolism and Weight Management

One of the key challenges faced by individuals with an endomorph body type is managing metabolism and weight effectively. The slower metabolism characteristic of endomorphs requires a strategic and personalized approach to maintaining a healthy weight and overall well-being.

Metabolic Rate:

Metabolism is the body's process of converting food into energy. Endomorphs typically have a slower metabolic rate, which means their bodies burn calories at a slower pace than other body types. This can contribute to easier weight gain, especially when calorie intake exceeds the calories burned through physical activity and basic bodily functions.

Caloric Intake and Energy Balance:

To manage weight effectively, endomorphs must pay careful attention to caloric intake and energy balance. Consuming more calories than the body needs for daily activities and functions leads to weight gain.

Balancing calorie intake with energy expenditure through exercise and physical activity is crucial for maintaining a healthy weight.

Dietary Considerations:

Endomorphs often benefit from a diet that focuses on nutrient-dense foods and portion control. Emphasizing whole foods, including fruits, vegetables, lean proteins, and whole grains, provides essential nutrients while helping control calorie intake. Portion control becomes particularly important to avoid overeating and manage weight effectively.

Strategic Exercise Routine:

Regular physical activity is essential for everyone, but for endomorphs, a strategic exercise routine takes on added significance. Combining cardiovascular exercises for calorie burning with strength training to build and maintain muscle mass is crucial. Muscle mass plays a role in increasing metabolic rate, aiding in weight management.

Consistency and Patience:

Weight management for endomorphs requires consistency and patience. Unlike quick-fix solutions, sustainable lifestyle changes are key to achieving and maintaining a healthy weight. Crash diets or extreme exercise regimens may not be suitable for endomorphs and can even be counterproductive. A gradual and balanced approach is more likely to yield long-term success.

Mindful Eating:

Practicing mindful eating is a valuable strategy for weight management. Being aware of hunger and fullness cues, savoring each bite, and avoiding distractions during meals contribute to a healthier relationship with food. This approach can help endomorphs make conscious choices and avoid overeating.

Hydration and Sleep:

Adequate hydration and quality sleep are often overlooked factors in weight management. Staying hydrated supports overall health and can help control appetite. Additionally, getting sufficient sleep is crucial, as sleep deprivation can impact metabolism and lead to increased cravings for unhealthy foods.

By understanding the unique metabolism and weight management challenges of the endomorph body type, individuals can develop a customized and sustainable approach to achieving and maintaining a healthy weight. It involves a combination of dietary choices, regular physical activity, and lifestyle adjustments that align with the characteristics of an endomorph.

3.3 Genetic Predispositions

Genetics plays a significant role in shaping an individual's body type, including whether they fall into the endomorph category. Understanding genetic predispositions is essential for making informed choices about health, fitness, and disease management.

Inheritance of Body Type:

The predisposition to be an endomorph, mesomorph, or ectomorph is largely inherited. Genes inherited from parents influence factors such as metabolism, fat storage, and muscle development. While genetics provide a blueprint, lifestyle choices and environmental factors also play a role in how these genetic traits manifest.

Impact on Weight and Fat Distribution:

Genetic factors contribute to an individual's tendency to gain or lose weight and the distribution of body fat. Endomorphs, influenced by genetic predispositions, may find it easier to gain weight and store fat, particularly in certain areas such as the abdomen and thighs. Understanding these genetic influences allows individuals to make choices that align with their unique body type.

Insights for Health Management:

Recognizing genetic predispositions provides valuable insights into potential health risks and strengths. For endomorphs, being aware of the tendency to store fat can inform proactive measures for weight management and the prevention of conditions like diabetes. It also underscores the importance of adopting a holistic approach that considers both genetic and lifestyle factors.

Interaction with Lifestyle Choices:

While genetics set the stage, lifestyle choices significantly influence how genetic traits are expressed. Even with a genetic predisposition to be an endomorph, adopting a healthy lifestyle can positively impact weight management, metabolism, and overall well-being. This includes making choices related to diet, physical activity, sleep, and stress management.

Tailoring Health Strategies:

Understanding genetic predispositions allows for the tailoring of health strategies to align with individual needs. For endomorphs, this might involve a more focused approach to weight management, including a balanced diet, regular exercise, and specific lifestyle adjustments. By acknowledging genetic influences, individuals can work towards optimizing their health within the parameters of their unique body type.

Prevention and Early Intervention:

Knowledge of genetic predispositions also aids in preventive healthcare and early intervention. For endomorphs with a family history of conditions like diabetes, proactive measures, such as regular screenings and lifestyle adjustments, become even more critical. Early intervention based on genetic risk factors can contribute to better health outcomes.

Genetic predispositions play a significant role in shaping the endomorph body type and influencing health outcomes. Rather than viewing genetics as deterministic, understanding these factors empowers individuals to make informed choices that align with their unique genetic makeup. It emphasizes the importance of a holistic and personalized approach to health and well-being that considers both genetic and environmental influences.

Living a Healthy Lifestyle

4.1 Nutrition for Endomorphs with Diabetes

Nutrition plays a pivotal role in managing diabetes for individuals with an endomorph body type. The combination of diabetes and an endomorphic tendency to store excess fat requires a thoughtful and strategic approach to dietary choices.

Balancing Macronutrients:

For endomorphs with diabetes, balancing macronutrients—carbohydrates, proteins, and fats—is crucial. While everyone with diabetes needs to monitor carbohydrate intake, endomorphs may need to pay extra attention due to their predisposition to weight gain. Choosing complex carbohydrates with a lower glycemic index, such as whole grains and legumes, can help manage blood sugar levels effectively.

Portion Control:

Endomorphs benefit significantly from practicing portion control to manage calorie intake. Eating smaller, well-balanced meals throughout the day helps prevent overeating and supports blood sugar stability. Including a variety of nutrient-dense foods in appropriate portions ensures a well-rounded and satisfying diet.

Lean Proteins:

Incorporating lean protein sources into meals is essential for endomorphs with diabetes. Protein not only supports muscle health but also helps in managing hunger and maintaining steady blood sugar levels. Sources of lean protein include poultry, fish, tofu, legumes, and low-fat dairy products.

Healthy Fats:

While endomorphs may tend to store excess fat, including healthy fats in the diet remains important for overall health. Opting for sources of unsaturated fats, such as avocados, nuts, seeds, and olive oil, can contribute to heart health and satiety without compromising blood sugar control.

Fiber-Rich Foods:

Dietary fiber plays a crucial role in managing blood sugar levels and promoting digestive health. Endomorphs with diabetes should prioritize fiber-rich foods, including fruits, vegetables, whole grains, and legumes. These foods provide essential nutrients and contribute to a feeling of fullness, supporting weight management efforts.

Hydration:

Staying hydrated is fundamental for overall health and diabetes management. Endomorphs with diabetes should prioritize water intake and limit sugary beverages. Adequate hydration supports kidney function, helps regulate blood sugar levels, and can contribute to weight management by preventing unnecessary calorie consumption from sugary drinks.

Meal Timing:

The timing of meals can impact blood sugar control for endomorphs with diabetes. Consistent meal timing helps regulate insulin levels and can contribute to better glycemic control. Eating at regular intervals throughout the day and avoiding large gaps between meals supports stable blood sugar levels.

Consultation with a Registered Dietitian:

Individualized guidance from a registered dietitian is invaluable for endomorphs managing diabetes. A dietitian can tailor dietary recommendations based on individual needs, preferences, and health goals. Regular consultations provide ongoing support, helping individuals make informed choices that align with both their diabetes management and endomorph body type.

In summary, nutrition for endomorphs with diabetes involves a balanced and thoughtful approach to macronutrients, portion control, and food choices. By focusing on nutrient-dense foods, adopting healthy eating habits, and seeking personalized guidance, individuals can effectively manage diabetes while addressing the unique characteristics of the endomorph body type.

4.2 Exercise and Physical Activity

Physical activity is a cornerstone of diabetes management for individuals with an endomorph body type. Regular exercise not only contributes to weight management but also plays a crucial role in improving insulin sensitivity and overall well-being.

Cardiovascular Exercise:

Endomorphs with diabetes benefit from incorporating cardiovascular exercises into their routine. Activities such as brisk walking, cycling, swimming, and dancing help burn calories, improve cardiovascular health, and contribute to weight management. Engaging in at least 150 minutes of moderate-intensity aerobic exercise per week is recommended for overall health.

Strength Training:

Including strength training exercises is particularly important for endomorphs. Building and maintaining muscle mass enhances metabolism, supporting weight management and blood sugar control. Strength training activities, such as weightlifting or resistance exercises, should be performed at least twice a week, targeting major muscle groups.

Flexibility and Balance:

Incorporating flexibility and balance exercises contributes to overall physical fitness and reduces the risk of injuries. Activities like yoga, tai chi, or stretching routines help maintain joint mobility and improve stability. These exercises, often overlooked, play a vital role in promoting long-term health for endomorphs with diabetes.

Individualized Approach:

Recognizing that each person is unique, an individualized approach to exercise is crucial. Endomorphs may find certain activities more enjoyable and sustainable, leading to greater adherence. Tailoring an exercise routine to individual preferences and fitness levels ensures a higher likelihood of incorporating physical activity into the daily routine.

Consistency and Gradual Progression:

Consistency is key when it comes to exercise for endomorphs with diabetes. Rather than opting for intense workouts that may be challenging to maintain, focusing on regular, moderate-intensity activities ensures a sustainable approach. Gradual progression in terms of duration and intensity allows the body to adapt without risking injury.

Monitoring Blood Sugar Levels:

For individuals with diabetes, monitoring blood sugar levels before and after exercise is essential. This practice provides insights into how different activities impact blood sugar and helps make informed decisions about adjustments in medication, food intake, or the timing of exercise. Collaborating with healthcare providers to develop a personalized plan for blood sugar management during exercise is recommended.

Enjoyable Activities:

Choosing activities that are enjoyable and align with personal interests increases the likelihood of adherence to an exercise routine. Whether it's dancing, hiking, or playing a sport, finding joy in physical activity makes it a sustainable part of daily life. This positive approach not only supports diabetes management but also contributes to overall mental and emotional well-being.

Consultation with Healthcare Professionals:

Before starting a new exercise regimen, individuals with diabetes, especially those with an endomorph body type, should consult with healthcare professionals. This ensures that the chosen activities are safe and appropriate for individual health conditions. Healthcare providers can offer guidance on adjusting medications, managing blood sugar during exercise, and addressing any specific concerns.

In conclusion, exercise is a vital component of diabetes management for endomorphs. By incorporating a mix of cardiovascular, strength, flexibility, and balance exercises into their routine, individuals can achieve holistic health benefits. An individualized and enjoyable approach to physical activity not only supports diabetes management but also contributes to a healthier and more fulfilling lifestyle.

4.3 Stress Management

Stress management is an integral aspect of maintaining overall health for individuals with an endomorph body type, especially when dealing with the challenges of diabetes. Chronic stress can have a significant impact on blood sugar levels and overall well-being.

Understanding the Stress-Diabetes Connection:

Stress activates the body's "fight or flight" response, leading to the release of stress hormones such as cortisol and adrenaline. While this response is essential in emergencies, chronic stress can result in prolonged elevation of these hormones, impacting blood sugar levels.

For individuals with diabetes, managing stress becomes crucial to maintain glycemic control.

Mindfulness and Relaxation Techniques:

Incorporating mindfulness and relaxation techniques into daily life can help manage stress effectively. Practices such as deep breathing, meditation, and progressive muscle relaxation promote a sense of calm and reduce the physiological effects of stress. These techniques are accessible and can be practiced anywhere, making them valuable tools for stress management.

Regular Physical Activity:

Physical activity not only contributes to weight management but also serves as a powerful stress-reducing tool. Engaging in regular exercise releases endorphins, the body's natural mood enhancers. Whether it's a brisk walk, a workout session, or a calming yoga practice, physical activity provides an outlet for stress and contributes to overall mental well-being.

Healthy Lifestyle Habits:

Adopting healthy lifestyle habits, including a balanced diet, regular exercise, and adequate sleep, creates a foundation for stress management. Ensuring proper nutrition, staying hydrated, and maintaining a consistent sleep schedule contribute to overall resilience in the face of stressors. These habits support both physical and mental health.

Social Support:

Maintaining strong social connections is a valuable resource for managing stress. Having a support system of friends, family, or support groups provides an outlet for sharing concerns, receiving encouragement, and fostering a sense of belonging. Social interactions contribute to emotional well-being and act as a buffer against the negative effects of stress.

Time Management and Prioritization:

Effectively managing time and prioritizing tasks contribute to reducing stress levels. Breaking tasks into manageable steps, setting realistic goals, and avoiding overcommitment are essential strategies. Learning to say no when necessary and delegating tasks can also contribute to a more balanced and stress-resistant lifestyle.

Professional Support:

For individuals struggling with chronic stress or its impact on diabetes management, seeking professional support is crucial. Mental health professionals, such as psychologists or counselors, can provide tools and strategies to cope with stress. Additionally, healthcare providers can offer guidance on managing diabetes in the context of stress and adjusting medications if needed.

Hobbies and Leisure Activities:

Engaging in hobbies and leisure activities provides a positive outlet for stress. Whether it's reading, gardening, art, or music, dedicating time to activities that bring joy and relaxation contributes to overall well-being. These activities act as a counterbalance to the demands of daily life and enhance resilience in the face of stressors.

Mind-Body Practices:

Mind-body practices, such as yoga and tai chi, combine physical activity with mindfulness, promoting relaxation and stress reduction. These practices integrate movement, breath awareness, and mental focus, fostering a holistic approach to well-being. Incorporating mind-body practices into a routine can enhance the body's ability to manage stress.

In summary, stress management is a vital component of maintaining health for individuals with an endomorph body type, particularly when managing diabetes. By adopting a multifaceted approach that includes mindfulness, physical activity, healthy lifestyle habits, social support, and professional guidance when needed, individuals can navigate stress more effectively and support overall well-being.

4.4 Importance of Adequate Sleep

Adequate sleep is often underestimated but plays a crucial role in the overall health of individuals with an endomorph body type, especially those managing diabetes. Quality sleep is essential for various bodily functions, including blood sugar regulation, metabolism, and overall well-being.

Sleep and Blood Sugar Regulation:

Sleep has a profound impact on blood sugar levels and insulin sensitivity. Inadequate or poor-quality sleep can lead to insulin resistance, making it more challenging for the body to regulate blood sugar. This, in turn, increases the risk of diabetes complications for individuals with diabetes, especially those with an endomorph body type.

Circadian Rhythm and Hormonal Balance:

The body's internal clock, known as the circadian rhythm, influences sleep-wake cycles and various physiological processes. Disruptions in the circadian rhythm, often caused by irregular sleep patterns, can impact hormonal balance, including the hormones that regulate appetite and blood sugar. Consistent and adequate sleep supports a healthy circadian rhythm.

Impact on Weight Management:

Sleep plays a vital role in weight management, a key consideration for endomorphs. Inadequate sleep can disrupt the balance of hunger hormones, leading to increased appetite and cravings for unhealthy foods. Over time, this can contribute to weight gain and the challenges associated with managing diabetes effectively.

Sleep Hygiene Practices:

Adopting good sleep hygiene practices contributes to better sleep quality. This includes maintaining a consistent sleep schedule, creating a comfortable sleep environment, and practicing a relaxing bedtime routine. Minimizing exposure to screens before bedtime and avoiding stimulants like caffeine in the evening are important aspects of promoting quality sleep.

Effects of Diabetes on Sleep:

The relationship between diabetes and sleep is bidirectional. While poor sleep can impact blood sugar control, the challenges of managing diabetes can also interfere with sleep. Fluctuations in blood sugar levels, discomfort from diabetic complications, and the need for nighttime monitoring can disrupt sleep patterns. Addressing both sleep-related issues and diabetes management is crucial for overall health.

Strategies for Better Sleep:

Developing strategies for better sleep is essential for individuals with an endomorph body type managing diabetes. This may involve creating a calming bedtime routine, optimizing the sleep environment, and addressing any specific sleep-related concerns. Seeking guidance from healthcare providers or sleep specialists can provide tailored solutions.

Regular Physical Activity and Sleep:

Engaging in regular physical activity supports both diabetes management and sleep quality. Exercise promotes the release of endorphins, contributing to a positive mood and reducing stress—factors that enhance sleep. Establishing a consistent exercise routine, ideally earlier in the day, can positively impact sleep patterns.

Professional Evaluation of Sleep Issues:

For individuals experiencing persistent sleep issues, seeking professional evaluation is important. Sleep disorders, such as sleep apnea or insomnia, may contribute to poor sleep quality. Healthcare providers can conduct assessments, recommend sleep studies if needed, and provide targeted interventions to address specific sleep-related challenges.

Importance of Sleep for Overall Well-being:

Recognizing that sleep is not just a luxury but a fundamental aspect of health is crucial. Adequate and restful sleep contributes to improved mood, cognitive function, and immune system function. It also supports the body's ability to recover and repair, which is particularly important for individuals managing chronic conditions like diabetes.

The importance of adequate sleep cannot be overstated, especially for individuals with an endomorph body type managing diabetes. Prioritizing quality sleep through consistent sleep hygiene practices, addressing sleep-related challenges, and seeking professional guidance when needed contribute to better overall health and diabetes management.

Managing Diabetes Medications

5.1 Oral Medications for Diabetes

Managing diabetes often involves a combination of lifestyle modifications and medications. Oral medications are a common and effective treatment option for individuals with diabetes, including those with an endomorph body type. Understanding the different classes of oral medications and how they work is essential for optimizing diabetes management.

Metformin:

Metformin is a widely prescribed oral medication for the treatment of Type 2 diabetes. It belongs to the class of medications known as biguanides and works by reducing glucose production in the liver and improving insulin sensitivity in the body's tissues. Metformin does not cause the pancreas to produce more insulin but helps the body use insulin more effectively.

Sulfonylureas:

Sulfonylureas are another class of oral medications commonly used to manage Type 2 diabetes. Examples include glyburide, glipizide, and glimepiride. Sulfonylureas stimulate the pancreas to release more insulin, helping lower blood sugar levels. It's important for individuals using sulfonylureas to be mindful of the risk of hypoglycemia, as these medications can cause blood sugar levels to drop too low.

Meglitinides:

Meglitinides, such as repaglinide and nateglinide, are oral medications that stimulate the release of insulin from the pancreas. They work quickly and are taken before meals to help control postprandial (after-meal) blood sugar levels. Like sulfonylureas, meglitinides carry a risk of hypoglycemia and should be used with caution, especially in individuals with unpredictable meal patterns.

Thiazolidinediones (TZDs):

Thiazolidinediones, including pioglitazone and rosiglitazone, improve insulin sensitivity in the body's cells and reduce glucose production in the liver. TZDs are often prescribed for individuals with Type 2 diabetes who may not achieve optimal blood sugar control with other medications. However, they are associated with potential side effects, such as weight gain and an increased risk of heart issues, requiring careful consideration and monitoring.

Dipeptidyl Peptidase-4 (DPP-4) Inhibitors:

DPP-4 inhibitors, like sitagliptin and saxagliptin, work by increasing the levels of incretin hormones, which stimulate insulin release and inhibit glucagon secretion. This class of medications is taken orally and is generally well-tolerated. They are often prescribed as part of a comprehensive treatment plan for individuals with Type 2 diabetes.

Sodium-Glucose Cotransporter-2 (SGLT2) Inhibitors:

SGLT2 inhibitors, such as canagliflozin and empagliflozin, target the kidneys to reduce the reabsorption of glucose and increase its excretion through urine. This class of medications helps lower blood sugar levels and may also have additional cardiovascular and renal benefits. However, individuals using SGLT2 inhibitors need to be monitored for potential side effects, including urinary tract infections and an increased risk of diabetic ketoacidosis.

Combination Medications:

Combination medications combine two or more classes of oral diabetes medications into a single pill. This approach simplifies the medication regimen for individuals with diabetes, enhancing adherence and convenience. Common combinations include metformin with sulfonylureas or DPP-4 inhibitors. The choice of combination therapy depends on individual factors such as blood sugar control, side effect profiles, and patient preferences.

Considerations for Endomorphs:

Individuals with an endomorph body type may face specific challenges related to weight management, which should be considered when selecting oral diabetes medications. Metformin, with its potential for weight neutrality or even modest weight loss, is often a favorable option. However, medications associated with weight gain, such as thiazolidinediones, may need careful consideration, and alternative options might be explored in collaboration with healthcare providers.

Regular monitoring of blood sugar levels, along with open communication with healthcare providers, is crucial for adjusting and optimizing oral diabetes medication regimens. Lifestyle modifications, including a balanced diet and regular physical activity, complement the effects of these medications and contribute to overall diabetes management.

5.2 Insulin Therapy

Insulin therapy is a crucial component of diabetes management, especially for individuals with an endomorph body type who may have insulin resistance or impaired insulin function. Understanding the different types of insulin, administration methods, and individualized insulin regimens is essential for optimizing blood sugar control.

Types of Insulin:

There are several types of insulin, categorized based on their onset, peak, and duration of action. These include:

- **Rapid-Acting Insulin:** Begins working within 15 minutes, peaks in about an hour, and lasts for 2 to 4 hours. Examples include insulin lispro, insulin aspart, and insulin glulisine.

- **Short-Acting Insulin:** Starts working within 30 to 60 minutes, peaks in 2 to 3 hours, and has a duration of 3 to 6 hours. Regular insulin falls into this category.

- **Intermediate-Acting Insulin:** Onset is 2 to 4 hours, peak is 4 to 12 hours, and duration is 12 to 18 hours. NPH (Neutral Protamine Hagedorn) insulin is an example.

- **Long-Acting Insulin:** Has a slow onset, little to no peak, and a long duration of action. Examples include insulin glargine, insulin detemir, and insulin degludec.

- **Ultra-Long-Acting Insulin:** Provides a prolonged and steady release of insulin over an extended period. Insulin degludec falls into this category.

Insulin Administration Methods:

Insulin can be administered through various methods, and the choice depends on individual preferences, lifestyle, and healthcare provider recommendations.

- **Insulin Injections:** Administered subcutaneously using syringes, insulin pens, or insulin pumps. Subcutaneous injections involve injecting insulin into the fatty tissue just under the skin. The choice of injection method is often influenced by factors such as ease of use, discretion, and personal preference.

- **Insulin Pumps:** Small devices that deliver a continuous supply of insulin through a small tube placed under the skin. Insulin pumps mimic the function of a healthy pancreas more closely and allow for precise insulin dose adjustments. They are particularly beneficial for individuals with variable insulin needs.

- **Inhalable Insulin:** An alternative to injections, inhalable insulin delivers insulin in a powdered form through the lungs. It is a rapid-acting insulin option and may be suitable for certain individuals who prefer an inhalable option.

Individualized Insulin Regimens:

Creating an individualized insulin regimen is crucial for achieving optimal blood sugar control. Factors such as lifestyle, daily routines, meal patterns, and activity levels influence the timing and dosage of insulin. Healthcare providers work collaboratively with individuals to tailor insulin regimens, taking into account both the type and method of insulin administration.

Combination Therapy:

For some individuals, a combination of oral medications and insulin may be prescribed to achieve better blood sugar control. This approach is particularly relevant for individuals with Type 2 diabetes who may experience progression in the severity of their condition over time.

Considerations for Endomorphs:

Individuals with an endomorph body type may be more prone to insulin resistance, where the body's cells do not respond effectively to insulin. This can necessitate higher insulin doses or more intensive insulin regimens. Lifestyle modifications, including regular physical activity and a balanced diet, play a crucial role in supporting insulin sensitivity.

Regular monitoring of blood sugar levels, along with ongoing communication with healthcare providers, is essential for adjusting and optimizing insulin regimens. Flexibility in the insulin regimen allows for adaptations based on factors such as changes in activity levels, meal patterns, and overall health.

5.3 Monitoring and Adjusting Medications

Monitoring blood sugar levels and making necessary adjustments to medications are fundamental aspects of diabetes management. Regular self-monitoring of blood glucose (SMBG) or continuous glucose monitoring (CGM) provides valuable insights into how well medications are working and helps guide adjustments to achieve optimal blood sugar control.

Self-Monitoring of Blood Glucose (SMBG):

SMBG involves regularly checking blood sugar levels using a blood glucose meter. This method allows individuals to assess their current blood sugar levels at different times of the day, typically before meals and at bedtime. By tracking these values, individuals can identify patterns, understand how various factors influence blood sugar, and make informed decisions about medication adjustments.

Continuous Glucose Monitoring (CGM):

CGM systems provide real-time data on blood sugar levels throughout the day and night. These systems use a sensor inserted under the skin to measure glucose levels in the interstitial fluid. The information is transmitted to a device or smartphone, allowing individuals to see trends, set alerts for high or low blood sugar, and make timely adjustments to their diabetes management plan.

Hemoglobin A1c Testing:

Hemoglobin A1c (HbA1c) is a blood test that provides an average of blood sugar levels over the past two to three months. It measures the percentage of hemoglobin that is glycated, or bound to glucose. HbA1c testing is a valuable tool for assessing overall blood sugar control and the effectiveness of diabetes management. Healthcare providers use this information to make adjustments to medication regimens.

Individualized Targets:

Setting individualized blood sugar targets is a collaborative process between individuals with diabetes and their healthcare providers. Factors such as age, overall health, presence of other medical conditions, and individual preferences influence the target ranges for blood sugar levels. These targets serve as a guide for medication adjustments and lifestyle modifications.

Adjustments to Oral Medications:

For individuals taking oral medications, adjustments may involve changes in dosage, timing, or the addition of new medications. Regular monitoring of blood sugar levels helps identify if the current medication regimen effectively controls glucose levels. Healthcare providers may make adjustments based on the individual's response to medications and changes in lifestyle.

Adjustments to Insulin Therapy:

Insulin regimens may require frequent adjustments to align with changes in lifestyle, activity levels, and overall health. Regular blood sugar monitoring helps individuals and healthcare providers identify patterns and make informed decisions about insulin dosage, timing, or the type of insulin used. Adjustments may be necessary to address fluctuations in blood sugar levels throughout the day.

Collaborative Approach:

Effective monitoring and adjustments to diabetes medications require a collaborative approach between individuals and their healthcare providers. Regular communication, open discussions about lifestyle changes, and a willingness to share information about blood sugar patterns contribute to a more personalized and effective diabetes management plan.

Lifestyle Modifications:

In addition to medication adjustments, lifestyle modifications play a crucial role in achieving optimal blood sugar control. Changes in diet, physical activity, stress management, and sleep patterns can significantly impact blood sugar levels. Individuals and healthcare providers work together to create realistic and sustainable lifestyle strategies that complement medication adjustments.

Education and Empowerment:

Empowering individuals with diabetes through education on monitoring and medication adjustments is essential. Understanding the rationale behind medication changes, recognizing the impact of lifestyle choices, and feeling confident in using monitoring devices contribute to active and informed self-management.

Regular Healthcare Visits:

Regular visits to healthcare providers are essential for ongoing monitoring and adjustments to diabetes medications. These visits provide an opportunity to discuss any challenges, review blood sugar trends, and make collaborative decisions about medication regimens. They also allow for preventive care, addressing potential complications, and optimizing overall health.

Monitoring blood sugar levels and making necessary adjustments to medications are integral components of effective diabetes management. Whether through self-monitoring of blood glucose, continuous glucose monitoring, or hemoglobin A1c testing, the insights gained support informed decision-making and contribute to personalized and optimized diabetes care. Regular collaboration with healthcare providers, along with a commitment to lifestyle modifications, empowers individuals to navigate the dynamic nature of diabetes and achieve long-term well-being.

Meal Planning for Endomorphs

6.1 Balanced and Nutrient-Rich Diets

For individuals with an endomorph body type, meal planning is a key aspect of managing both diabetes and weight. Crafting balanced and nutrient-rich diets that prioritize essential nutrients, control calorie intake, and manage blood sugar levels is crucial. Understanding the components of a balanced diet and making informed food choices contribute to overall health and well-being.

Foundations of a Balanced Diet:

A balanced diet encompasses a variety of food groups, ensuring that the body receives a wide range of essential nutrients. Key components include:

1. **Fruits and Vegetables:** These are rich in vitamins, minerals, fiber, and antioxidants. They contribute to overall health, support digestive function, and provide essential nutrients for managing diabetes.

2. **Whole Grains:** Whole grains, such as brown rice, quinoa, and whole wheat, are excellent sources of fiber and complex carbohydrates. They provide sustained energy, support digestive health, and help regulate blood sugar levels.

3. **Lean Proteins:** Protein is essential for muscle health, satiety, and blood sugar control. Opting for lean protein sources, including poultry, fish, tofu, legumes, and low-fat dairy, contributes to a well-rounded diet.

4. **Healthy Fats:** Including sources of healthy fats, such as avocados, nuts, seeds, and olive oil, supports heart health and provides a sense of satiety. While individuals with an endomorph body type may be mindful of fat intake, incorporating these healthy fats is essential.

5. **Dairy or Dairy Alternatives:** These provide calcium and vitamin D, crucial for bone health. Choosing low-fat or non-fat options helps manage calorie and fat intake.

6. **Balanced Carbohydrates:** Selecting complex carbohydrates with a lower glycemic index, such as whole grains, legumes, and vegetables, supports blood sugar control. Monitoring carbohydrate intake is particularly important for individuals with diabetes.

Calorie Control and Weight Management:

Endomorphs may tend to gain weight more easily, making calorie control a crucial aspect of meal planning. While the focus is on nutrient-rich foods, portion control is essential to manage overall calorie intake. Creating a calorie deficit, where the calories consumed are slightly less than those expended, supports weight management goals.

Fiber-Rich Foods:

Incorporating fiber-rich foods into meals is beneficial for endomorphs in managing diabetes. Fiber promotes feelings of fullness, supports digestive health, and helps regulate blood sugar levels. Fruits, vegetables, whole grains, and legumes are excellent sources of dietary fiber.

Hydration:

Staying adequately hydrated is often overlooked but is a fundamental aspect of a balanced diet. Water supports overall health, aids digestion, and can contribute to a feeling of fullness. Choosing water as the primary beverage and limiting sugary drinks aligns with diabetes management and weight control goals.

Individualized Approaches:

Recognizing that each person is unique, an individualized approach to meal planning is crucial. Factors such as age, gender, activity level, and personal preferences influence dietary needs. Consulting with a registered dietitian can provide personalized guidance, taking into account both diabetes management and the endomorph body type.

Meal Ideas:

Creating balanced meals can be enjoyable and varied. Here are some meal ideas for individuals with an endomorph body type managing diabetes:

- **Breakfast:** Whole grain oats topped with berries and a sprinkle of nuts, accompanied by a side of Greek yogurt.

- **Lunch:** Grilled chicken or tofu salad with a mix of colorful vegetables, quinoa, and a light vinaigrette dressing.

- **Dinner:** Baked salmon with roasted sweet potatoes and steamed broccoli.

- **Snacks:** Sliced apple with almond butter, a handful of cherry tomatoes with hummus, or a small portion of mixed nuts.

Continuous Monitoring and Adjustments:

Meal planning for endomorphs managing diabetes is not a static process. Continuous monitoring of blood sugar levels, along with regular adjustments to the diet, is necessary. Understanding how different foods impact blood sugar and being proactive in making informed choices contribute to effective diabetes management.

6.2 Portion Control Strategies

Portion control is a critical component of meal planning for individuals with an endomorph body type managing diabetes. Controlling portion sizes helps regulate calorie intake, manage blood sugar levels, and support weight management goals. Implementing effective portion control strategies involves mindful eating, awareness of serving sizes, and finding a balance that aligns with individual needs.

Understanding Serving Sizes:

One of the first steps in portion control is understanding recommended serving sizes for different food groups. While nutritional labels provide information, visual cues can also help. For example, a serving of meat is roughly the size of a deck of cards, a cup of vegetables is about the size of a baseball, and a medium piece of fruit is comparable to a tennis ball.

Use of Portion Control Tools:

Portion control tools, such as measuring cups, food scales, and visual guides, can be valuable aids. Measuring out specific portions during meal preparation helps individuals become more aware of their intake and provides a tangible reference for appropriate serving sizes. Over time, this practice can become intuitive.

Choose Smaller Plates and Bowls:

Opting for smaller plates and bowls can create an illusion of a fuller plate, promoting satisfaction with smaller portions. This visual trick can be particularly helpful for individuals who find it challenging to adjust to reduced portion sizes.

Mindful Eating Practices:

Mindful eating involves being fully present and attentive during meals. Paying attention to hunger and fullness cues, savoring each bite, and eating without distractions can enhance awareness of portion sizes. This practice promotes a healthier relationship with food and helps prevent overeating.

Pre-Portioning Snacks:

Pre-portioning snacks into individual servings can prevent mindless eating and support portion control. Instead of eating directly from a large bag or container, dividing snacks into smaller portions helps manage calorie intake and encourages conscious choices.

Listen to Hunger and Fullness Signals:

Listening to the body's hunger and fullness signals is a fundamental aspect of portion control. Eating when hungry and stopping when satisfied, rather than when overly full, promotes a balanced approach to meals. Recognizing the difference between physical hunger and emotional cues supports mindful eating.

Include a Variety of Foods:

Incorporating a variety of foods into meals not only enhances nutritional intake but also contributes to a satisfying eating experience. Including a mix of vegetables, proteins, whole grains, and healthy fats provides a well-rounded meal that supports portion control and overall health.

Be Mindful of Liquid Calories:

Liquid calories, such as those from sugary beverages or high-calorie drinks, can contribute significantly to overall calorie intake. Being mindful of liquid calories and opting for water, herbal teas, or other low-calorie beverages supports both weight management and blood sugar control.

Practice Moderation, Not Deprivation:

Portion control is about moderation, not deprivation. Enjoying favorite foods in smaller portions allows for satisfaction without compromising health goals. Restrictive diets can be challenging to maintain and may lead to feelings of deprivation, making it more difficult to sustain healthy eating habits.

Consultation with a Registered Dietitian:

For individuals with diabetes and an endomorph body type, seeking guidance from a registered dietitian is invaluable. A dietitian can provide personalized strategies for portion control, taking into account individual dietary preferences, cultural considerations, and diabetes management goals. This collaborative approach ensures a sustainable and effective meal plan.

Meal Planning Apps:

Technology can be a helpful tool in practicing portion control. Various meal-planning apps provide features such as tracking food intake, monitoring portion sizes, and offering nutritional information. These tools can enhance awareness of eating habits and support individuals in making informed choices.

6.3 Meal Timing and Frequency

The timing and frequency of meals play a significant role in blood sugar management, especially for individuals with an endomorph body type managing diabetes. Establishing a regular meal schedule, understanding the impact of meal timing on blood sugar levels, and incorporating healthy snacks contribute to overall glucose control.

Establishing a Regular Meal Schedule:

Consistency in meal timing is essential for individuals with diabetes. Establishing a regular meal schedule helps regulate blood sugar levels, as the body becomes accustomed to the timing of food intake. Aim for three balanced meals per day with evenly spaced snacks if needed.

Impact of Meal Timing on Blood Sugar:

The timing of meals influences blood sugar levels and how the body responds to insulin. Spreading meals throughout the day helps prevent large fluctuations in blood sugar, supporting more stable levels. It also allows the body to use insulin more effectively, improving overall glucose control.

Balancing Carbohydrates Across Meals:

Distributing carbohydrate intake evenly across meals helps manage blood sugar levels throughout the day. This approach prevents spikes or crashes in glucose and supports a more steady release of insulin.

Including a mix of complex carbohydrates, proteins, and healthy fats in each meal contributes to balanced nutrition.

The Role of Snacks:

For individuals with diabetes, well-timed snacks can be a valuable tool in managing blood sugar levels. Healthy snacks between meals help prevent hypoglycemia (low blood sugar) and support a more consistent energy supply. Opt for nutrient-dense snacks, such as a small handful of nuts, yogurt with berries, or sliced vegetables with hummus.

Consideration of Meal Composition:

Understanding how different foods impact blood sugar is crucial when planning meal timing. Meals with a moderate to low glycemic index, which release glucose more slowly into the bloodstream, can be particularly beneficial. Additionally, combining carbohydrates with proteins and healthy fats can further support stable blood sugar levels.

Meal Timing Around Medication:

For individuals taking diabetes medications, the timing of meals is often coordinated with medication schedules. This is especially relevant for those using insulin or certain oral medications that require alignment with meal times. Consistent communication with healthcare providers helps ensure that meal timing aligns with medication effectiveness.

Adjusting Meal Timing for Physical Activity:

Incorporating physical activity into the daily routine may require adjustments to meal timing. Eating a balanced meal or snack before exercise can help provide energy and prevent low blood sugar. Post-exercise meals should support recovery and replenish glycogen stores. Coordination between meal planning and physical activity is essential for optimal glucose control.

Listening to Hunger and Fullness Cues:

In addition to adhering to a regular meal schedule, paying attention to hunger and fullness cues supports mindful eating. Eating when hungry and stopping when satisfied promotes a healthy relationship with food and prevents overeating. This approach aligns with both blood sugar management and weight control goals.

Hydration Between Meals:

Staying hydrated between meals is important for overall health and can contribute to a feeling of fullness. Drinking water throughout the day helps prevent dehydration and supports optimal bodily functions. Opting for water or other low-calorie beverages aligns with both diabetes management and weight control.

Meal Timing and Circadian Rhythms:

The body's internal clock, known as the circadian rhythm, influences various physiological processes, including metabolism and insulin sensitivity. Aligning meal timing with circadian rhythms may have additional benefits for blood sugar control. For example, eating larger meals earlier in the day and lighter meals in the evening may align with the body's natural patterns.

Individualized Approach:

Recognizing that each person's schedule, preferences, and lifestyle are unique, an individualized approach to meal timing is essential. Collaborating with a registered dietitian or healthcare provider can help tailor meal timing strategies to align with both diabetes management goals and the individual's routine.

Meal planning for individuals with an endomorph body type managing diabetes involves creating balanced and nutrient-rich diets, implementing effective portion control strategies, and considering the timing and frequency of meals. These components work synergistically to support blood sugar control, weight management, and overall well-being. Continuous monitoring, adjustments based on individual needs, and collaboration with healthcare professionals contribute to a sustainable and effective meal plan for individuals with diabetes and an endomorph body type.

Fitness Strategies for Endomorphs with Diabetes

7.1 Tailoring Exercise Routines

For individuals with an endomorph body type managing diabetes, tailoring exercise routines is a crucial aspect of achieving overall health and well-being. Recognizing the unique characteristics of an endomorph body type, including a tendency to store excess fat and potential challenges in weight management, allows for the creation of effective and sustainable fitness strategies.

Understanding the Endomorph Body Type:

Endomorphs typically have a rounder or softer physique, with a tendency to store fat more easily than other body types. This genetic predisposition can make weight management a particular focus when designing exercise routines. However, it's essential to approach fitness with a holistic mindset, considering not only weight but also overall health, cardiovascular fitness, and blood sugar control.

Collaboration with Healthcare Providers:

Before embarking on any exercise routine, especially for individuals with diabetes, collaboration with healthcare providers is essential. Medical professionals can guide safe exercise practices, taking into account individual health conditions, medications, and potential risks. This collaborative approach ensures that fitness strategies align with overall diabetes management goals.

Individualized Exercise Plans:

Recognizing that each individual is unique, the development of individualized exercise plans is crucial. Factors such as fitness level, existing health conditions, personal preferences, and accessibility to exercise facilities contribute to tailoring routines that are both effective and enjoyable. This personalized approach enhances adherence and long-term success.

Incorporating Varied Activities:

Variety in exercise routines not only prevents monotony but also engages different muscle groups and energy systems. Cardiovascular activities, strength training, flexibility exercises, and recreational activities can be integrated to create a well-rounded fitness plan. This approach ensures a comprehensive approach to health and fitness.

Gradual Progression:

For individuals with diabetes and an endomorph body type, gradual progression in exercise intensity is key. Starting with low-impact activities and gradually increasing intensity allows the body to adapt and reduces the risk of injury. This approach is especially important for those new to regular physical activity or returning after a period of inactivity.

Monitoring Blood Sugar Levels:

Regular monitoring of blood sugar levels before, during, and after exercise provides valuable insights into how the body responds to different activities. This information helps individuals and healthcare providers make informed decisions about adjusting medications, timing meals, or modifying exercise routines to optimize blood sugar control.

7.2 Cardiovascular Activities

Cardiovascular activities are fundamental for individuals with an endomorph body type managing diabetes. These exercises not only contribute to weight management but also enhance cardiovascular health, improve insulin sensitivity, and support overall well-being. Tailoring cardiovascular activities to the unique characteristics of an endomorph body type ensures effectiveness and sustainability.

Benefits of Cardiovascular Exercise:

Cardiovascular or aerobic exercise offers a range of benefits for individuals with diabetes and an endomorph body type:

1. **Weight Management:** Engaging in regular cardiovascular activities helps burn calories and supports weight management, a key consideration for endomorphs.

2. **Improved Insulin Sensitivity:** Cardiovascular exercise enhances the body's sensitivity to insulin, facilitating better blood sugar control.

3. **Heart Health:** Aerobic activities strengthen the heart, improve circulation, and contribute to cardiovascular health.

4. **Mood Enhancement:** Cardiovascular exercise releases endorphins, the body's natural mood enhancers, contributing to improved mental well-being.

5. **Stress Reduction:** Regular aerobic activities help reduce stress levels, which is particularly important for individuals managing diabetes.

Tailoring Cardiovascular Activities for Endomorphs:

Tailoring cardiovascular activities to the unique characteristics of an endomorph body type involves considering factors such as joint health, preferences, and potential challenges in mobility. Here are some effective cardiovascular exercises for endomorphs managing diabetes:

1. **Walking:** A low-impact and accessible activity, walking is an excellent choice for endomorphs. It can be done outdoors or on a treadmill, allowing for customization based on fitness levels.

2. **Cycling:** Whether on a stationary bike or a traditional bicycle, cycling provides a cardiovascular workout with minimal impact

on the joints. It can be adapted to different fitness levels and preferences.

3. **Swimming:** Swimming and water aerobics are gentle on the joints, making them suitable for individuals with joint concerns. The buoyancy of water reduces impact while providing an effective cardiovascular workout.

4. **Elliptical Training:** Elliptical machines offer a low-impact alternative to traditional running or jogging. They engage both the upper and lower body, providing a full-body workout.

5. **Dance:** Engaging in dance, whether through structured classes or at-home routines, combines cardiovascular exercise with enjoyment. Dance can be adapted to different styles and intensities.

6. **Rowing:** Rowing machines provide a full-body workout, engaging the arms, legs, and core. The low-impact nature of rowing is beneficial for individuals with joint considerations.

Frequency and Duration:

The American Heart Association recommends at least 150 minutes of moderate-intensity aerobic exercise or 75 minutes of vigorous-intensity exercise per week, spread throughout the week. For individuals managing diabetes, distributing this exercise across most days enhances blood sugar control.

Interval Training:

Interval training involves alternating between periods of higher intensity and lower intensity or rest. This approach can be particularly effective for endomorphs managing diabetes, as it enhances cardiovascular fitness, promotes weight loss, and may improve insulin sensitivity.

Monitoring Blood Sugar During Cardiovascular Exercise:

Regular monitoring of blood sugar levels during cardiovascular exercise is essential. This practice helps individuals understand how different activities impact blood sugar and allows for adjustments in medication, food intake, or exercise intensity as needed. It's advisable to carry a glucose monitor or snacks for quick adjustments during exercise.

Collaboration with Healthcare Providers:

Before initiating or modifying a cardiovascular exercise routine, individuals with diabetes should consult their healthcare providers. Healthcare professionals can provide personalized recommendations based on individual health conditions, medications, and overall fitness levels. This collaborative approach ensures that cardiovascular activities align with diabetes management goals.

7.3 Strength Training for Endomorphs

Strength training is a vital component of fitness strategies for individuals with an endomorph body type managing diabetes. Building and maintaining muscle mass not only supports weight management but also enhances insulin sensitivity, bone health, and overall functional capacity. Tailoring strength training exercises to the specific needs of endomorphs ensures a well-rounded and effective fitness plan.

Benefits of Strength Training:

Incorporating strength training into a fitness routine offers numerous benefits for individuals with an endomorph body type managing diabetes:

1. **Muscle Mass Maintenance:** Strength training helps prevent muscle loss, especially important for individuals with diabetes who may be at risk of sarcopenia (age-related muscle loss).

2. **Weight Management:** Building lean muscle mass contributes to a higher resting metabolic rate, supporting weight management efforts for endomorphs.

3. **Improved Insulin Sensitivity:** Resistance training enhances insulin sensitivity, aiding in better blood sugar control.

4. **Bone Health:** Strength training is beneficial for bone health, reducing the risk of osteoporosis and fractures.

5. **Functional Fitness:** Strong muscles contribute to improved functional capacity, making daily activities easier and reducing the risk of falls.

Tailoring Strength Training for Endomorphs:

When tailoring strength training exercises for individuals with an endomorph body type, considerations include joint health, potential limitations, and preferences. Here are effective strength training exercises for endomorphs managing diabetes:

1. **Bodyweight Exercises:** Exercises such as squats, lunges, push-ups, and planks use the body's weight for resistance. These exercises can be adapted to different fitness levels and are gentle on the joints.

2. **Resistance Band Workouts:** Resistance bands provide variable resistance and are suitable for individuals with joint concerns. They can be used for a wide range of exercises targeting different muscle groups.

3. **Dumbbell or Kettlebell Exercises:** Incorporating dumbbells or kettlebells into a strength training routine adds resistance and challenges the muscles. Exercises may include bicep curls, shoulder presses, and kettlebell swings.

4. **Weight Machines:** Utilizing weight machines at the gym provides controlled resistance for various muscle groups.

Beginners can start with machines that offer guided movements and stability.

5. **Functional Movements:** Incorporating functional movements, such as squats, deadlifts, and rows, engages multiple muscle groups and supports overall strength and stability.

6. **Balance Exercises:** Including balance exercises, such as single-leg stands or stability ball exercises, enhances core strength and stability. This is particularly relevant for overall functional fitness.

Frequency and Progression:

The American College of Sports Medicine recommends strength training exercises for all major muscle groups at least two days per week. Gradual progression in intensity, repetitions, or resistance ensures ongoing muscle development and prevents plateaus in fitness gains.

Warm-Up and Cool Down:

Prioritizing warm-up and cool-down routines is crucial in strength training to prepare the muscles for exercise and promote flexibility. Dynamic stretches, light cardio, and mobility exercises can be incorporated into the warm-up, while static stretches and relaxation techniques are suitable for the cool-down.

Monitoring Blood Sugar During Strength Training:

While strength training may not lead to the same immediate blood sugar fluctuations as cardiovascular exercise, it's essential to monitor blood sugar levels, especially for individuals with diabetes. Factors such as stress and the intensity of the workout can influence blood sugar. Regular monitoring helps individuals make informed decisions about medication, food intake, or adjustments to the strength training routine.

Progressive Overload:

To continue seeing improvements in strength and muscle mass, progressive overload is essential. This involves gradually increasing the intensity, resistance, or duration of strength training exercises. Whether through added weight, increased repetitions, or advanced variations, progressive overload challenges the muscles and promotes ongoing development.

Consultation with Healthcare Providers:

Individuals with diabetes, especially those managing other health conditions, should consult their healthcare providers before initiating or modifying a strength training routine. Healthcare professionals can provide guidance on safe practices, potential modifications based on individual health considerations, and strategies to address specific concerns.

Integration with Cardiovascular Exercise:

A well-rounded fitness plan for individuals with an endomorph body type managing diabetes includes both cardiovascular activities and strength training. Combining these components provides comprehensive benefits for weight management, blood sugar control, and overall health. An integrated approach ensures a balanced and sustainable fitness routine.

Fitness strategies for endomorphs with diabetes involve tailoring exercise routines to address the unique characteristics of the endomorph body type. This includes cardiovascular activities to enhance cardiovascular health and weight management, as well as strength training to build and maintain muscle mass. A collaborative approach with healthcare providers, individualized plans, and a focus on gradual progression contributes to the effectiveness and sustainability of fitness strategies for individuals with an endomorph body type managing diabetes.

Coping with Challenges

8.1 Emotional Well-being

Coping with diabetes as an endomorph involves not only physical aspects but also emotional well-being. The interplay between the management of blood sugar levels, lifestyle adjustments, and the emotional toll of living with a chronic condition can be significant. Addressing emotional well-being is crucial for overall health and quality of life.

Understanding the Emotional Impact of Diabetes:

A diabetes diagnosis can bring a range of emotions, including shock, fear, anxiety, and even grief. Individuals with an endomorph body type may face additional challenges, such as concerns about weight management and body image. It's essential to acknowledge and validate these emotions, recognizing that the psychological aspect of diabetes is integral to overall well-being.

Open Communication:

Establishing open communication channels with healthcare providers, friends, and family is a key step in addressing emotional well-being. Sharing concerns, fears, and challenges fosters a support system that can provide guidance and understanding. Healthcare providers can offer resources, such as counseling or support groups, to further assist in managing the emotional aspects of diabetes.

Seeking Professional Support:

Managing the emotional impact of diabetes may involve seeking support from mental health professionals. Psychologists, counselors, or therapists with experience in chronic conditions can offer strategies for coping with stress, anxiety, and emotional challenges. Professional support provides a safe space to explore feelings and develop coping mechanisms.

Building a Support Network:

Building a strong support network is vital for emotional well-being. Friends, family, and peers who understand the challenges of diabetes can provide empathy, encouragement, and practical assistance. Sharing experiences and learning from others who have navigated similar emotional journeys can be empowering.

Mind-Body Techniques:

Incorporating mind-body techniques into daily life can significantly impact emotional well-being. Practices such as mindfulness meditation, deep breathing exercises, and yoga promote relaxation, reduce stress, and enhance overall mental health. These techniques are accessible and can be tailored to individual preferences and comfort levels.

Setting Realistic Goals:

Setting realistic and achievable goals is essential for managing emotional well-being. Rather than aiming for perfection, individuals can focus on gradual improvements in blood sugar control, lifestyle modifications, and emotional resilience. Celebrating small victories contributes to a positive mindset and a sense of accomplishment.

Educating Loved Ones:

Educating loved ones about diabetes, its emotional impact, and how they can provide support fosters understanding and empathy. Encouraging open conversations about the challenges and successes associated with diabetes creates a supportive environment. Loved ones can play a crucial role in the emotional well-being of individuals managing diabetes.

Monitoring Negative Thought Patterns:

It's common for individuals with diabetes to experience negative thought patterns related to their condition. These may include feelings of guilt, self-blame, or a sense of being overwhelmed. Identifying and challenging negative thoughts, perhaps with the help of a mental health professional, can contribute to a more positive and resilient mindset.

Addressing Body Image Concerns:

For endomorphs, concerns about body image and weight management may be heightened. Addressing these concerns involves recognizing that health is multifaceted and extends beyond physical appearance. Embracing a holistic view of well-being, including emotional and mental health, contributes to a more positive relationship with one's body.

Community Engagement:

Engaging with the diabetes community, either locally or online, provides a sense of belonging and shared experience. Participating in support groups, forums, or social media communities allows individuals to connect with others facing similar challenges. Peer support fosters a sense of community and reduces feelings of isolation.

Regular Check-ins with Healthcare Providers:

Regular check-ins with healthcare providers go beyond physical health assessments—they also provide an opportunity to discuss emotional well-being. Sharing feelings and concerns related to diabetes allows healthcare providers to offer guidance, resources, and potential adjustments to the overall diabetes management plan.

8.2 Dealing with Fluctuating Blood Sugar

Managing fluctuating blood sugar levels is a central challenge for individuals with diabetes, and endomorphs may encounter unique considerations in this regard. Understanding the factors that contribute to blood sugar fluctuations and developing effective coping strategies are crucial for maintaining optimal health.

Factors Influencing Blood Sugar Fluctuations:

Several factors can contribute to fluctuations in blood sugar levels, and recognizing these variables is the first step in managing them:

1. **Diet and Nutrition:** The types and amounts of food consumed directly impact blood sugar levels. Understanding the glycemic index of foods and monitoring carbohydrate intake helps individuals make informed dietary choices.

2. **Physical Activity:** Exercise has a direct effect on blood sugar levels. Engaging in physical activity can either lower or raise blood sugar, depending on the intensity and duration of the exercise.

3. **Medications:** The timing and dosage of diabetes medications, including insulin, play a crucial role in blood sugar control. Changes in medication regimens may lead to fluctuations.

4. **Stress Levels:** Stress activates the body's "fight or flight" response, releasing hormones that can raise blood sugar levels. Chronic stress can contribute to persistent fluctuations.

5. **Illness or Infection:** Illness or infection can cause an increase in blood sugar levels. Managing diabetes during times of illness may require adjustments to medication and increased monitoring.

6. **Hormonal Changes:** Hormonal fluctuations, particularly in women, can impact blood sugar levels. This includes menstrual cycles, pregnancy, and menopause.

Continuous Blood Sugar Monitoring:

Continuous monitoring of blood sugar levels provides real-time information about how the body responds to various factors. Continuous glucose monitoring (CGM) systems offer a continuous stream of data, allowing individuals to identify patterns, make timely adjustments, and gain insights into the impact of different lifestyle factors.

Individualized Blood Sugar Targets:

Setting individualized blood sugar targets in collaboration with healthcare providers is essential. Factors such as age, overall health, and the presence of other medical conditions influence target ranges. Striving for personalized targets supports a more realistic and achievable approach to blood sugar management.

Consistent Carbohydrate Monitoring:

Monitoring carbohydrate intake is a fundamental aspect of blood sugar control, especially for individuals with diabetes. Consistent monitoring of the types and amounts of carbohydrates consumed helps individuals make informed decisions about meal planning and insulin dosages.

Adjusting Insulin Regimens:

Endomorphs with diabetes may be more prone to insulin resistance, requiring adjustments to insulin regimens. Collaborating with healthcare providers to assess insulin sensitivity, making timely adjustments to dosages, and exploring different types of insulin contribute to optimal blood sugar management.

Hydration and Blood Sugar Control:

Staying adequately hydrated is important for overall health and may impact blood sugar levels. Dehydration can lead to higher blood sugar concentrations, emphasizing the importance of regular hydration as part of diabetes management.

Emergency Preparedness:

Being prepared for potential blood sugar emergencies, such as hypoglycemia (low blood sugar) or hyperglycemia (high blood sugar), is crucial. Having a plan in place, carrying necessary supplies, and educating loved ones on emergency procedures contribute to effective management.

Regular Healthcare Visits:

Regular healthcare visits provide opportunities for comprehensive assessments of blood sugar management. These visits allow healthcare providers to review blood sugar trends, make adjustments to medication regimens, and address any challenges or concerns related to fluctuating blood sugar levels.

Education on Hypoglycemia and Hyperglycemia:

Education on the signs, symptoms, and management of hypoglycemia and hyperglycemia is vital. Recognizing early warning signs and knowing how to respond in different situations empowers individuals to take prompt action and seek assistance if needed.

Support Systems for Blood Sugar Management:

Building a strong support system is crucial for managing blood sugar fluctuations. Loved ones, friends, and colleagues can assist with episodes of low or high blood sugar. Educating those nearby about the necessary steps during emergencies enhances overall safety.

Psychosocial Impact of Blood Sugar Fluctuations:

The psychosocial impact of blood sugar fluctuations should not be underestimated. Individuals may experience feelings of frustration, anxiety, or stress when dealing with unpredictable blood sugar levels. Addressing the emotional aspects, possibly through counseling or support groups, complements physical management strategies.

Incorporating Technology:

Advancements in technology, such as smartphone apps and wearable devices, offer tools for tracking and managing blood sugar levels. These technologies can provide real-time alerts, trend analysis, and insights that support individuals in making informed decisions about their diabetes management.

8.3 Overcoming Setbacks

Living with diabetes as an endomorph involves navigating a journey marked by successes and challenges. Overcoming setbacks is an integral part of this journey, requiring resilience, adaptability, and a proactive approach to managing both the physical and emotional aspects of diabetes.

Understanding Setbacks:

Setbacks in diabetes management can manifest in various forms, including unexplained changes in blood sugar levels, difficulty adhering to a healthy lifestyle, or encountering obstacles in treatment plans. Recognizing setbacks as part of the overall journey allows individuals to approach them with a problem-solving mindset.

Reframing Challenges as Learning Opportunities:

Viewing setbacks as learning opportunities rather than failures is a constructive mindset. Each challenge provides insights into potential adjustments needed in diabetes management strategies, whether related to diet, medication, exercise, or emotional well-being.

Establishing Realistic Expectations:

Setting realistic expectations is crucial for overcoming setbacks. Diabetes management is a dynamic process, and there will be times when blood sugar levels may deviate from target ranges. Establishing realistic expectations helps individuals navigate setbacks without feelings of discouragement.

Regular Review of Diabetes Management Plan:

Periodic reviews of the diabetes management plan with healthcare providers ensure that the plan remains effective and aligned with individual goals. Adjustments may be necessary based on changes in health, lifestyle, or other influencing factors.

Collaboration with Healthcare Providers:

Maintaining open communication with healthcare providers during setbacks is essential. Discussing challenges, concerns, and potential adjustments to the treatment plan allows for a collaborative approach to overcoming setbacks. Healthcare providers can offer guidance and support to navigate challenges effectively.

Strategies for Overcoming Dietary Setbacks:

Dietary setbacks, such as deviations from meal plans or overindulgence, are common challenges. Implementing strategies to overcome these setbacks include:

1. **Mindful Eating:** Practicing mindful eating involves being present during meals, savoring each bite, and paying attention to hunger and fullness cues. This approach supports a healthier relationship with food.

2. **Meal Planning:** Planning meals in advance helps individuals make intentional choices and reduces the likelihood of impulsive or unhealthy eating.

3. **Nutrition Education:** Enhancing nutrition knowledge provides individuals with the tools to make informed choices, understand the impact of different foods on blood sugar, and create balanced and satisfying meals.

4. **Seeking Support:** Engaging with a registered dietitian or nutritionist for support and guidance during setbacks can be valuable. These professionals can offer personalized advice and strategies for managing dietary challenges.

Strategies for Overcoming Physical Activity Setbacks:

Setbacks in physical activity, whether due to illness, injury, or lifestyle changes, can impact diabetes management. Strategies for overcoming physical activity setbacks include:

1. **Adapting Exercise Routines:** If facing limitations or setbacks in regular exercise, adapting routines to accommodate current abilities is essential. This may involve choosing lower-impact activities or incorporating modified exercises.

2. **Gradual Reintroduction:** Following a period of inactivity, gradually reintroducing physical activity helps prevent injuries and allows the body to adapt. Starting with low-intensity exercises and increasing gradually reduces the risk of setbacks.

3. **Alternative Activities:** Exploring alternative activities that align with individual preferences and physical capabilities ensures ongoing engagement in regular physical activity. This could include swimming, yoga, or other forms of exercise that are gentler on the body.

4. **Setting Realistic Goals:** Adjusting exercise goals based on current health status and abilities prevents feelings of frustration. Setting achievable goals encourages consistency and helps overcome setbacks more effectively.

Strategies for Overcoming Emotional Setbacks:

Emotional setbacks, such as stress, anxiety, or feelings of overwhelm, can impact overall well-being. Strategies for overcoming emotional setbacks include:

1. **Mind-Body Practices:** Incorporating mind-body practices, such as meditation, deep breathing, or mindfulness, helps manage stress and promotes emotional well-being.

2. **Counseling or Therapy:** Seeking counseling or therapy provides a safe space to explore and address emotional challenges. Mental health professionals can offer strategies for coping with stressors related to diabetes.

3. **Expressive Arts:** Engaging in expressive arts, such as journaling, art, or music, provides a creative outlet for expressing and processing emotions associated with setbacks.

4. **Support Groups:** Participating in diabetes support groups or connecting with peers who share similar experiences fosters a sense of community and reduces feelings of isolation.

5. **Self-Compassion:** Practicing self-compassion involves treating oneself with kindness and understanding during challenging times. Acknowledging that setbacks are a part of the journey and expressing self-compassion contributes to resilience.

Strategies for Overcoming Medication Setbacks:

Issues related to medication, such as missed doses or side effects, can present setbacks in diabetes management. Strategies for overcoming medication setbacks include:

1. **Medication Adherence Tools:** Utilizing tools such as medication reminders, pill organizers, or smartphone apps supports consistent medication adherence.

2. **Communication with Healthcare Providers:** Open communication with healthcare providers about any challenges or concerns related to medications allows for timely adjustments or alternative solutions.

3. **Education on Medications:** Understanding the purpose, dosage, and potential side effects of medications enhances

informed decision-making and empowers individuals to manage medications effectively.

4. **Collaboration with Pharmacists:** Consulting with pharmacists can provide additional guidance on medication management, potential interactions, and strategies for overcoming challenges.

Strategies for Overcoming Lifestyle Setbacks:

Lifestyle setbacks, such as disruptions in routines or challenges in incorporating healthy habits, can impact diabetes management. Strategies for overcoming lifestyle setbacks include:

1. **Flexible Planning:** Adopting a flexible approach to lifestyle planning allows for adjustments based on changing circumstances. Flexibility enables individuals to navigate unexpected challenges without feeling overwhelmed.

2. **Goal Setting:** Setting realistic and achievable lifestyle goals supports ongoing adherence to healthy habits. Small, incremental changes contribute to long-term success.

3. **Mindful Decision-Making:** Practicing mindful decision-making involves being intentional about choices related to food, physical activity, and overall well-being. Mindfulness supports awareness and empowers individuals to make conscious decisions.

4. **Celebrating Progress:** Acknowledging and celebrating progress, no matter how small, reinforces positive behavior and encourages continued efforts toward a healthy lifestyle.

Developing a Resilient Mindset:

Cultivating a resilient mindset involves embracing challenges as opportunities for growth, learning, and adaptation. Resilience enables individuals to bounce back from setbacks, maintain a positive outlook, and approach diabetes management with a proactive attitude.

Celebrating Successes:

Amidst the challenges of living with diabetes, celebrating successes is paramount. Whether achieving blood sugar targets, making positive lifestyle changes, or overcoming setbacks, recognizing and celebrating successes contributes to motivation and a sense of accomplishment.

Coping with challenges in diabetes management as an endomorph involves addressing emotional well-being, developing strategies for dealing with fluctuating blood sugar, and cultivating resilience to overcome setbacks. The integration of physical and emotional strategies, collaboration with healthcare providers, and a proactive approach to setbacks contribute to a holistic and effective approach to living with diabetes.

Support Systems

9.1 Building a Healthcare Team

Building a comprehensive healthcare team is a cornerstone for individuals with diabetes, especially those who identify as endomorphs. The complexity of diabetes management requires collaboration with a diverse group of healthcare professionals to address various aspects of physical and emotional well-being.

Diabetes Educators:

Diabetes educators play a pivotal role in empowering individuals with the knowledge and skills needed to manage diabetes effectively. These professionals, often nurses or dietitians specializing in diabetes education, provide personalized guidance on meal planning, blood sugar monitoring, medication management, and lifestyle modifications. Building a relationship with a diabetes educator ensures ongoing support and education tailored to individual needs.

Endocrinologists:

Endocrinologists specialize in hormonal and metabolic disorders, making them key members of a diabetes healthcare team. These medical professionals can assess overall health, manage medications, and provide guidance on insulin therapy. Regular consultations with an endocrinologist are essential for adjusting treatment plans, addressing complications, and ensuring comprehensive diabetes care.

Primary Care Physicians:

Primary care physicians play a central role in managing overall health and coordinating care for individuals with diabetes. They monitor blood pressure, cholesterol levels, and other vital health indicators, addressing both diabetes-related and general health concerns. An effective partnership with a primary care physician ensures integrated and holistic healthcare.

Registered Dietitians:

Nutrition is a crucial aspect of diabetes management, and registered dietitians specialize in providing personalized dietary guidance. Working with a registered dietitian helps individuals develop balanced and nutritious meal plans, manage weight, and make informed food choices. The collaboration supports sustainable lifestyle changes that contribute to overall health and blood sugar control.

Pharmacists:

Pharmacists are valuable members of the healthcare team, particularly in managing diabetes medications. They provide information on medication interactions, potential side effects, and optimal medication adherence. Regular communication with pharmacists ensures that individuals understand their medications, address concerns, and receive guidance on proper usage.

Podiatrists:

Foot care is a significant consideration for individuals with diabetes, and podiatrists specialize in the health of the feet. Regular foot examinations, preventive care, and prompt intervention for any foot-related issues are crucial to prevent complications. Incorporating podiatrists into the healthcare team supports overall diabetes care and reduces the risk of foot-related complications.

Ophthalmologists:

Regular eye examinations are essential for individuals with diabetes to monitor for any diabetic retinopathy or other eye-related complications. Ophthalmologists specialize in eye health and can detect and manage issues early, preserving vision and preventing severe complications. Integrating regular eye check-ups into the diabetes management routine is essential.

Mental Health Professionals:

The emotional impact of living with diabetes is significant, and mental health professionals, including psychologists or counselors, can provide essential support. These professionals help individuals navigate the emotional challenges associated with diabetes, develop coping strategies, and address any mental health concerns. Collaboration with mental health professionals contributes to a holistic approach to diabetes care.

Physical Therapists:

Physical therapists play a role in maintaining overall physical health, addressing mobility concerns, and preventing or managing complications related to diabetes. They can provide tailored exercise programs, address musculoskeletal issues, and support individuals in maintaining an active lifestyle. Collaboration with physical therapists enhances the overall well-being of individuals with diabetes.

Social Workers:

Social workers contribute to the holistic care of individuals with diabetes by addressing social and environmental factors that may impact health. They can assist with access to resources, navigate healthcare systems, and provide support for emotional and practical challenges. Building a relationship with a social worker ensures a comprehensive approach to diabetes management.

Regular Check-ins and Communication:

Establishing regular check-ins with each member of the healthcare team is essential for ongoing diabetes care. Open communication allows individuals to discuss any concerns, provide updates on their health status, and receive guidance on adjustments to their diabetes management plan. Collaborative decision-making ensures that all aspects of diabetes care are addressed comprehensively.

Coordination Among Healthcare Providers:

Effective coordination among healthcare providers is crucial to ensure that the care provided is well-integrated and aligned with individual health goals. Healthcare professionals should communicate regularly, share relevant information, and coordinate care plans to provide seamless and comprehensive support for individuals with diabetes.

Patient Advocacy:

Being an active advocate for one's health is a key aspect of building a healthcare team. Individuals should feel empowered to communicate their needs, ask questions, and actively participate in decision-making about their diabetes care. A collaborative approach between individuals and their healthcare team fosters a strong partnership focused on achieving optimal health outcomes.

9.2 Connecting with Other Endomorphs with Diabetes

Connecting with others who share similar experiences, especially those who identify as endomorphs with diabetes, can provide valuable support, encouragement, and a sense of community. Shared experiences create a unique bond and foster a supportive environment for navigating the challenges and celebrating successes associated with diabetes management.

Online Diabetes Communities:

The digital age has brought forth numerous online platforms and communities dedicated to diabetes support. Joining online forums, and social media groups, or participating in virtual discussions allows individuals to connect with other endomorphs with diabetes from around the world. These platforms provide a space for sharing experiences, seeking advice, and offering encouragement.

Local Support Groups:

Local diabetes support groups offer an opportunity for face-to-face interactions with individuals who share similar challenges. These groups may be organized by healthcare facilities, community centers, or diabetes advocacy organizations. Regular meetings, guest speakers, and group activities create a supportive and informative environment.

Endomorph-Specific Resources:

Seeking out resources and information specifically tailored to endomorphs with diabetes can provide targeted guidance. This may include books, websites, or articles that address the unique considerations and challenges faced by individuals with an endomorph body type. These resources can offer practical tips, success stories, and motivation.

Diabetes Conferences and Events:

Attending diabetes conferences and events provides an opportunity to connect with a diverse community of individuals managing diabetes. These gatherings often feature workshops, presentations by healthcare professionals, and networking opportunities. Engaging with others in person fosters a sense of camaraderie and shared commitment to diabetes well-being.

Peer Mentorship Programs:

Peer mentorship programs pair individuals with experienced mentors who have successfully navigated diabetes management. Having a mentor who understands the specific challenges faced by endomorphs with diabetes can provide personalized guidance, motivation, and a supportive connection. Peer mentorship creates a positive and empowering dynamic.

Collaborative Wellness Initiatives:

Engaging in collaborative wellness initiatives with other endomorphs with diabetes can be both enjoyable and beneficial. This could include group exercise classes, cooking workshops, or other activities that promote a healthy lifestyle. Shared experiences in these initiatives contribute to a sense of community and mutual support.

Personalized Support Networks:

Building personalized support networks with individuals who understand the nuances of managing diabetes as an endomorph is invaluable. Whether through friendships, online connections, or local groups, having a network of understanding individuals creates a strong foundation for navigating the journey of diabetes management.

Sharing Success Stories:

Sharing success stories within the endomorph community serves as inspiration and motivation. Individuals can celebrate achievements, whether related to blood sugar control, weight management, or overall well-being. These success stories reinforce the idea that positive outcomes are achievable and contribute to a positive mindset.

Advocacy for Endomorph-Specific Needs:

Being part of a community allows individuals to collectively advocate for endomorph-specific needs in diabetes care. This may involve raising awareness, seeking research on the intersection of endomorph body types and diabetes, and advocating for inclusive healthcare practices that address the unique challenges faced by this group.

Creating Safe Spaces:

Establishing safe spaces within the community, whether online or in-person, ensures that individuals feel comfortable sharing their experiences and seeking support. Safe spaces foster open dialogue, empathy, and a non-judgmental atmosphere where individuals can express their challenges and triumphs.

9.3 Family and Friends Support

Family and friends play a crucial role in the support system of individuals with diabetes, providing emotional encouragement, practical assistance, and a sense of connectedness. Nurturing these relationships and fostering understanding among loved ones contribute to a positive and empowering environment for diabetes management.

Education and Awareness:

Educating family and friends about diabetes, especially within the context of an endomorph body type, is essential. Providing information about the condition, its management, and specific considerations for endomorphs creates a foundation for supportive relationships. Awareness reduces misconceptions and fosters a shared understanding of the challenges involved.

Involving Loved Ones in Diabetes Care:

Involving loved ones in aspects of diabetes care, such as meal planning, exercise routines, or medication support, strengthens the sense of teamwork. Collaborating on healthy lifestyle choices creates a supportive environment that extends beyond individual efforts. Loved ones can contribute to creating a diabetes-friendly home environment.

Open Communication:

Establishing open communication channels with family and friends is crucial. Individuals with diabetes should feel comfortable discussing their needs, concerns, and successes with their loved ones. Open communication fosters empathy, allows for mutual understanding, and enables loved ones to offer appropriate support.

Attending Healthcare Appointments Together:

Inviting family members or close friends to attend healthcare appointments provides them with insights into diabetes management. Attending appointments together allows healthcare providers to address questions, clarify information, and involve loved ones in the collaborative aspect of diabetes care.

Participating in Diabetes Education Programs:

Joining diabetes education programs together with family members or friends enhances collective knowledge and skills in diabetes management. These programs often cover various aspects of diabetes care, including nutrition, physical activity, and emotional well-being. Shared learning experiences contribute to a supportive and informed network.

Empowering Loved Ones to Recognize Diabetes Signs:

Empowering loved ones to recognize signs of hypo or hyperglycemia and understanding appropriate responses is crucial. This knowledge enables family and friends to provide timely assistance during potential emergencies, contributing to overall safety and well-being.

Acknowledging Emotional Impact:

Recognizing and acknowledging the emotional impact of diabetes on both individuals and their loved ones is essential. Diabetes management can be emotionally challenging, and family and friends may also experience stress or concern. Open discussions about emotions and mutual support contribute to a resilient support system.

Celebrating Milestones and Achievements:

Celebrating milestones and achievements, whether related to blood sugar control, lifestyle changes, or other aspects of diabetes management, reinforces a positive and encouraging atmosphere. Acknowledging successes, no matter how small, creates a sense of accomplishment and motivates continued efforts.

Encouraging Healthy Lifestyle Changes as a Group:

Encouraging healthy lifestyle changes as a group fosters a collective commitment to well-being. This could involve family-friendly exercise activities, cooking nutritious meals together, or engaging in shared wellness initiatives. Group involvement creates a supportive environment that benefits everyone involved.

Addressing Concerns and Misconceptions:

Family and friends may have concerns or misconceptions about diabetes, especially in the context of an endomorph body type. Openly addressing concerns, providing accurate information, and dispelling myths contribute to a supportive and informed social network.

Respecting Individual Choices:

Respecting individual choices in diabetes management is crucial. While loved ones can offer support and encouragement, individuals with diabetes should feel empowered to make decisions that align with their preferences and health goals. Mutual respect fosters a trusting and positive support system.

Providing Emotional Support During Challenges:

Offering emotional support during challenging times, such as fluctuations in blood sugar levels, medication adjustments, or lifestyle changes, is a key role for family and friends. Providing a listening ear, offering encouragement, and being empathetic contribute to a strong and resilient support system.

Creating a Diabetes-Friendly Environment:

Creating a diabetes-friendly environment at home involves making adjustments to support healthy habits. This may include stocking nutritious foods, encouraging physical activity, and creating spaces for relaxation and stress management. A supportive environment contributes to the overall well-being of individuals with diabetes.

Participating in Wellness Activities Together:

Engaging in wellness activities together, such as family walks, cooking healthy meals, or practicing relaxation techniques, strengthens bonds and promotes a shared commitment to health. Participating in activities that contribute to overall well-being creates positive experiences and lasting memories.

Building a robust support system for individuals with diabetes, especially those who identify as endomorphs, involves collaboration with a diverse healthcare team, connecting with others who share similar experiences, and fostering understanding and support within the family and friend circle. A well-rounded support system contributes to a positive and empowering environment for navigating the complexities of diabetes management.

Success Stories

10.1 Inspiring Accounts of Endomorphs Thriving with Diabetes

The journey of living with diabetes as an endomorph comes with its unique set of challenges, but numerous inspiring accounts showcase that thriving with diabetes is not only possible but can be a remarkable journey of resilience, determination, and positive transformations.

Personal Narratives of Successful Blood Sugar Control:

One of the most compelling success stories within the diabetes community involves individuals who have successfully managed and controlled their blood sugar levels. Endomorphs, with their specific metabolic characteristics, share narratives of achieving and maintaining optimal blood sugar control through a combination of lifestyle modifications, medication adherence, and regular monitoring. These stories not only inspire but also provide valuable insights into the strategies that have proven effective for others facing similar challenges.

Weight Management Success Stories:

Endomorphs often face additional considerations when it comes to weight management in the context of diabetes. Success stories of individuals who have achieved and sustained healthy weight levels while effectively managing diabetes serve as beacons of inspiration. These narratives shed light on the importance of a balanced diet, regular physical activity, and the development of sustainable habits for maintaining a healthy weight, all while navigating the complexities of diabetes.

Incorporating Fitness into Daily Life:

Integrating fitness into daily life is a significant achievement for individuals with diabetes, and success stories highlight the transformative power of regular exercise. Endomorphs share their experiences of overcoming obstacles, starting with achievable fitness routines, and gradually progressing to more advanced activities. These narratives emphasize the positive impact of physical activity on blood sugar management, overall health, and the emotional well-being of individuals living with diabetes.

Achieving Diabetes Management Goals:

Success stories within the endomorph diabetes community often revolve around individuals achieving specific diabetes management goals. Whether it's reaching target HbA1c levels, mastering the art of carbohydrate counting, or consistently following a medication regimen, these accounts demonstrate that setting and attaining personalized goals is an integral part of thriving with diabetes. Personal victories contribute to a sense of empowerment and control over one's health.

Balancing Nutrition for Optimal Health:

Nutrition plays a pivotal role in diabetes management, and success stories from endomorphs highlight the importance of balanced and mindful eating. Individuals share their journeys of discovering nutritious food choices, mastering portion control and developing a positive relationship with food. These narratives provide practical insights into creating sustainable, diabetes-friendly meal plans that prioritize both health and enjoyment.

Navigating Emotional Well-being:

The emotional impact of living with diabetes is profound, and success stories often include accounts of individuals navigating and overcoming emotional challenges. Endomorphs share their experiences of seeking support from mental health professionals, incorporating mindfulness practices into their daily routines, and building resilient mindsets. These narratives underscore the importance of addressing emotional well-being as a fundamental aspect of thriving with diabetes.

Overcoming Medication Challenges:

Success stories within the endomorph diabetes community also address the journey of overcoming challenges related to medications. Individuals share how they have successfully adhered to medication regimens, navigated adjustments, and found a personalized approach to insulin therapy. These stories encourage others facing similar medication-related obstacles, emphasizing the significance of collaboration with healthcare providers for optimal management.

Celebrating Lifestyle Transformations:

Lifestyle transformations encompass a spectrum of changes, from adopting healthier dietary habits to embracing regular exercise routines. Success stories highlight how endomorphs have celebrated these transformations, experiencing positive shifts in overall well-being. These narratives showcase the transformative impact of lifestyle changes on blood sugar control, weight management, and the overall quality of life for individuals with diabetes.

Thriving Despite Genetic Predispositions:

Genetic predispositions can present additional challenges for endomorphs managing diabetes, but success stories showcase that genetic factors do not determine destiny. Individuals share their journeys of thriving despite familial histories of diabetes, emphasizing the role of proactive health management, early intervention, and lifestyle choices in shaping positive outcomes. These narratives provide hope and inspiration for those grappling with genetic predispositions.

Empowering Advocacy and Community Engagement:

Some success stories extend beyond individual achievements to encompass advocacy and community engagement. Endomorphs who have become advocates for diabetes awareness, education, and support share their impactful journeys. These narratives underscore the power of community engagement in creating positive change, fostering support networks, and contributing to a collective voice for individuals with diabetes.

Building Resilience in the Face of Challenges:

Success stories often center around the resilience demonstrated by endomorphs facing diabetes-related challenges. From coping with fluctuating blood sugar levels to overcoming setbacks, these narratives highlight the strength and adaptability of individuals living with diabetes. Personal stories of resilience inspire others to face challenges with a positive mindset, reinforcing the belief that setbacks are part of the journey to thriving with diabetes.

10.2 Overcoming Obstacles and Achieving Health Goals

The journey of overcoming obstacles while striving to achieve health goals is a testament to the resilience, determination, and tenacity of individuals living with diabetes, particularly those who identify as endomorphs. These success stories exemplify the triumph over challenges and the pursuit of optimal health despite the complexities of diabetes management.

Navigating Weight-Related Challenges:

Endomorphs, with their specific body type characteristics, may encounter unique challenges related to weight management in the context of diabetes. Success stories narrate the journey of overcoming weight-related obstacles, such as insulin resistance and metabolic factors. Individuals share their strategies for achieving and maintaining a healthy weight, emphasizing the importance of a balanced lifestyle and personalized approaches to nutrition and exercise.

Overcoming Insulin Resistance:

Insulin resistance is a common challenge for endomorphs with diabetes, requiring tailored approaches to insulin therapy. Success stories shed light on how individuals have effectively managed and overcome insulin resistance through medication adjustments, lifestyle modifications, and collaboration with healthcare providers. These narratives provide insights into navigating the intricacies of insulin therapy for optimal blood sugar control.

Balancing Blood Sugar Levels:

Achieving and maintaining balanced blood sugar levels is a central goal for individuals with diabetes. Success stories within the endomorph community detail the strategies employed to navigate the nuances of blood sugar management. From adopting personalized meal plans to fine-tuning medication regimens, these narratives offer practical guidance and motivation for others striving to balance blood sugar levels effectively.

Overcoming Dietary Challenges:

Dietary challenges are an integral aspect of diabetes management, and success stories highlight how individuals have overcome obstacles related to food choices, portion control, and nutritional balance. Endomorphs share their experiences of navigating dietary challenges, implementing realistic and sustainable changes, and finding joy in a diabetes-friendly approach to eating. These stories inspire others to embrace a positive relationship with food while managing diabetes.

Embracing Physical Activity:

Incorporating regular physical activity into daily life is a key component of diabetes management, and success stories from endomorphs emphasize the transformative impact of exercise. Individuals share their journeys of overcoming barriers to physical activity, developing enjoyable fitness routines, and experiencing improvements in both physical and mental well-being. These narratives encourage others to find joy in movement and prioritize physical activity as a vital aspect of health.

Navigating Emotional Well-being:

Success stories often delve into the emotional aspects of living with diabetes, highlighting the challenges faced and the strategies employed to foster emotional well-being. Endomorphs share their experiences of navigating stress, anxiety, and the psychological impact of diabetes. These narratives provide insights into the importance of seeking support, practicing self-care, and developing resilient mindsets for optimal emotional health.

Overcoming Setbacks and Resilience:

Setbacks are an inevitable part of the diabetes journey, but success stories showcase the resilience demonstrated by individuals who have overcome setbacks and continued to pursue their health goals. These narratives detail the strategies for bouncing back from challenges, learning from setbacks, and maintaining a positive outlook. The stories of resilience inspire others to view setbacks as opportunities for growth and continued improvement.

Managing Medications Effectively:

Effectively managing diabetes medications is a critical aspect of overall health, and success stories within the endomorph community provide insights into navigating medication regimens. Individuals share their experiences of overcoming challenges related to medication adherence, adjusting dosages, and collaborating with healthcare providers to find optimal solutions. These narratives offer practical guidance for others facing similar medication-related obstacles.

Thriving Despite Genetic Factors:

Genetic factors can present additional complexities in diabetes management, but success stories highlight individuals who have thrived despite familial predispositions. Endomorphs share their journeys of proactive health management, early intervention, and the adoption of lifestyle changes to mitigate the impact of genetic factors.

These narratives empower others to take charge of their health and make positive choices despite genetic predispositions.

Celebrating Personal Health Milestones:

Success stories often include celebrations of personal health milestones, whether related to blood sugar control, weight management, or overall well-being. Endomorphs share their joy in achieving specific health goals, emphasizing the importance of setting realistic objectives and celebrating progress along the diabetes journey. These stories instill a sense of accomplishment and motivation for others to pursue their health milestones.

Inspiring Advocacy and Community Impact:

Some success stories extend beyond individual achievements to encompass advocacy and community impact. Endomorphs share their journeys of becoming advocates for diabetes awareness, education, and support, contributing to positive changes at the community level. These narratives underscore the transformative power of individual stories in creating awareness and fostering a supportive community for individuals living with diabetes.

Empowering Others Through Sharing Experiences:

One common thread in success stories is the empowerment of others through the sharing of personal experiences. Endomorphs share their journeys with the intent of inspiring, motivating, and providing practical insights for individuals facing similar challenges. These narratives create a sense of community, solidarity, and shared determination to overcome obstacles and achieve health goals.

Success stories within the endomorph diabetes community are powerful narratives of triumph over challenges, determination in pursuing health goals, and the transformative impact of lifestyle changes. These stories inspire, guide, and foster a sense of community among individuals living with diabetes, emphasizing that thriving is not only achievable but a continuous and empowering journey.

Future Trends and Innovations

11.1 Emerging Technologies in Diabetes Management

The landscape of diabetes management is continually evolving, driven by advancements in technology that aim to enhance monitoring, treatment, and overall well-being for individuals living with diabetes. As we look toward the future, several emerging technologies show promise in revolutionizing diabetes care, offering new avenues for personalized, efficient, and patient-centric approaches.

Continuous Glucose Monitoring (CGM) Innovations:

Continuous Glucose Monitoring (CGM) technology has significantly transformed how individuals monitor their blood glucose levels, providing real-time data for better decision-making. Future trends in CGM are expected to bring about enhancements in accuracy, usability, and integration with other health technologies. Innovations may include smaller and more discreet sensors, improved data-sharing capabilities, and advancements in predictive analytics for proactive diabetes management.

Artificial Intelligence (AI) in Diabetes Management:

The integration of Artificial Intelligence (AI) holds tremendous potential in diabetes management, offering personalized insights, decision support, and predictive analytics. AI algorithms can analyze vast amounts of data, including glucose levels, lifestyle patterns, and treatment responses, to provide tailored recommendations. Future trends may include AI-driven glucose prediction models, adaptive treatment algorithms, and smart insulin delivery systems.

Smart Insulin Pens and Pumps:

Smart insulin delivery devices are evolving to provide more precise and customizable insulin administration. Future innovations in insulin pens and pumps may incorporate connectivity features, enabling seamless integration with CGM systems and smartphone apps. Enhanced user interfaces, dose optimization algorithms, and improved accuracy in insulin delivery are anticipated trends in the development of smart insulin delivery solutions.

Telehealth and Remote Patient Monitoring:

The acceleration of telehealth and remote patient monitoring has been particularly pronounced in recent years, offering convenient and accessible healthcare solutions. Future trends in diabetes management may see further integration of telehealth platforms, enabling individuals to consult with healthcare providers, receive personalized guidance, and remotely monitor their health. Virtual clinics and telemedicine apps may become integral components of diabetes care.

Wearable Health Technologies:

The wearable technology market is expanding rapidly, with wearables offering a range of health monitoring capabilities. For diabetes management, future trends may include more advanced wearable devices that not only track glucose levels but also monitor additional health parameters. Integration with fitness trackers, smartwatches, and other wearables can provide a holistic view of an individual's health and support proactive diabetes management.

Personalized Medicine and Genetic Therapies:

Advancements in genetics and personalized medicine are influencing the development of targeted therapies for diabetes. Future trends may involve the exploration of genetic markers associated with diabetes risk and response to specific treatments. Personalized medicine approaches can lead to tailored interventions that consider an individual's genetic predispositions, optimizing treatment effectiveness and minimizing potential side effects.

Implantable Devices for Long-Term Monitoring:

Implantable devices are emerging as potential solutions for long-term glucose monitoring and insulin delivery. Future trends may include the development of small, implantable sensors that can provide continuous glucose readings without the need for external devices. Implantable insulin delivery systems with closed-loop capabilities are also being explored as a means to automate insulin administration based on real-time glucose levels.

Digital Therapeutics and Mobile Apps:

The rise of digital therapeutics and mobile applications in diabetes management is expected to continue, with a focus on delivering evidence-based interventions and support. Future trends may involve more sophisticated digital therapeutics that offer personalized coaching, behavioral interventions, and cognitive support. Mobile apps may integrate with wearable devices to provide real-time feedback and facilitate proactive self-management.

Blockchain Technology for Secure Data Management:

As the importance of secure and interoperable health data becomes increasingly evident, blockchain technology is gaining attention in the healthcare sector. Future trends may see the adoption of blockchain for secure and transparent management of diabetes-related data. This includes the secure sharing of health records, ensuring data integrity, and facilitating collaborative research efforts while maintaining individual privacy.

Innovations in Non-Invasive Glucose Monitoring:

The pursuit of non-invasive methods for glucose monitoring remains a focal point in diabetes research. Future trends may involve innovations in non-invasive technologies such as optical sensors, sweat-based glucose monitoring, and breath analysis. These technologies aim to provide a more comfortable and convenient alternative to traditional fingerstick methods for monitoring blood glucose levels.

Integration of Smart Technology in Diabetes Education:

Educational resources and self-management support are integral components of diabetes care. Future trends may involve the integration of smart technology, including virtual reality (VR) and augmented reality (AR), to enhance diabetes education. Immersive experiences and interactive simulations can provide individuals with hands-on learning opportunities, improving their understanding of diabetes management principles.

Regulatory and Reimbursement Advancements:

The landscape of healthcare regulation and reimbursement is evolving to accommodate emerging technologies in diabetes management. Future trends may involve streamlined regulatory pathways for innovative devices, ensuring faster market access. Additionally, advancements in reimbursement models may encourage the adoption of digital health solutions, making them more accessible to a broader population.

Environmental and Contextual Data Integration:

A holistic approach to diabetes management involves considering environmental and contextual factors that impact an individual's health. Future trends may involve the integration of environmental data, such as air quality and weather conditions, with diabetes management platforms. This contextual information can provide additional insights into how external factors influence blood glucose levels and overall well-being.

Interoperability and Data Sharing Initiatives:

The importance of interoperability in healthcare cannot be overstated, and future trends in diabetes management may see increased efforts to establish standardized data-sharing protocols. Interoperable systems enable seamless communication between different devices and platforms, fostering collaborative care and empowering individuals to share their health data securely with healthcare providers.

Environmental Sustainability in Diabetes Technologies:

As the field of diabetes technology advances, considerations for environmental sustainability are gaining prominence. Future trends may involve the development of eco-friendly materials, energy-efficient devices, and responsible manufacturing practices within the diabetes technology sector. Sustainable innovations aim to minimize the environmental impact of diabetes management solutions.

In conclusion, the future of diabetes management is poised to witness remarkable transformations driven by emerging technologies. From advancements in continuous glucose monitoring to the integration of artificial intelligence and the exploration of personalized genetic therapies, these innovations hold the promise of improving the lives of individuals with diabetes. As technology continues to evolve, the focus remains on creating more accessible, personalized, and efficient solutions that empower individuals to take control of their diabetes journey.

11.2 Research and Developments for Endomorphs

Understanding the unique characteristics and challenges associated with the endomorph body type in the context of diabetes management has spurred dedicated research efforts. Ongoing developments aim to tailor interventions, treatments, and support mechanisms specifically for individuals who identify as endomorphs. Exploring these research initiatives provides insights into the future landscape of diabetes care for this specific population.

Endomorph-Specific Genetic Studies:

Research into the genetic factors influencing diabetes risk and progression in individuals with an endomorph body type is a crucial area of exploration. Future developments may involve comprehensive genetic studies that identify specific gene variants associated with diabetes in endomorphs. Understanding the genetic basis can inform targeted interventions and personalized treatment approaches.

Metabolic Profiling and Biomarker Discovery:

Metabolic profiling aims to characterize the unique metabolic signatures of endomorphs with diabetes. Researchers are exploring biomarkers that can provide insights into metabolic dysregulation, insulin resistance, and other factors specific to the endomorph body type. Biomarker discovery holds the potential to refine diagnostic approaches and guide personalized treatment strategies.

Precision Nutrition for Endomorphs:

The intersection of nutrition and the endomorph body type in the context of diabetes management is an area of active research. Future developments may involve precision nutrition approaches that take into account the metabolic characteristics of endomorphs. Tailored dietary interventions, considering factors such as nutrient absorption and metabolism, aim to optimize blood glucose control for individuals with diabetes.

Endomorph-Specific Clinical Trials:

Incorporating endomorph-specific considerations into clinical trial design is crucial for generating evidence-based recommendations. Researchers may conduct clinical trials specifically focused on interventions for diabetes management in endomorphs. These trials can assess the effectiveness of medications, lifestyle interventions, and technological solutions with a targeted approach to the endomorph body type.

Behavioral Interventions and Endomorph Psychology:

Understanding the behavioral aspects and psychological factors influencing diabetes management in endomorphs is an evolving area of research. Future developments may involve tailored behavioral interventions that address the unique challenges and motivations of individuals with the endomorph body type. Psychosocial support and strategies to enhance adherence to lifestyle modifications can be key components of these interventions.

Advancements in Endomorph-Specific Medications:

Research into medications that specifically target the metabolic characteristics of endomorphs is a promising avenue. Future developments may include the exploration of medications designed to address insulin resistance, optimize weight management, and improve overall metabolic health in individuals with the endomorph body type. These advancements aim to provide more targeted and effective treatment options.

Personalized Exercise Prescriptions for Endomorphs:

Exercise is a cornerstone of diabetes management, and ongoing research is focused on tailoring exercise prescriptions for individuals with the endomorph body type. Future developments may involve personalized exercise recommendations that consider factors such as metabolism, body composition, and cardiovascular health specific to endomorphs. These prescriptions aim to optimize the benefits of physical activity in diabetes care.

Integration of Technology for Endomorph-Specific Monitoring:

The integration of technology in monitoring and managing diabetes is advancing, and future developments may include solutions specifically designed for endomorphs. This could involve the customization of continuous glucose monitoring (CGM) systems, wearable devices, and health apps to account for the unique physiological characteristics and challenges associated with the endomorph body type.

Understanding Gut Microbiota in Endomorphs with Diabetes:

The role of gut microbiota in metabolic health is a burgeoning area of research, and investigations specific to endomorphs with diabetes are underway. Future developments may uncover the relationships between gut microbiota composition, metabolic factors, and diabetes outcomes in individuals with the endomorph body type. Insights from these studies can inform targeted interventions to modulate gut health.

Psychosocial Support Strategies for Endomorphs:

Recognizing the psychosocial dimensions of diabetes management for endomorphs, researchers are exploring strategies to enhance emotional well-being and mental health. Future developments may involve interventions such as cognitive-behavioral therapies, support groups, and digital mental health tools tailored to the specific needs and challenges faced by individuals with the endomorph body type.

Environmental and Lifestyle Interventions for Endomorphs:

Research into the environmental and lifestyle factors influencing diabetes risk and outcomes in endomorphs is an evolving field. Future developments may include interventions that address aspects such as sedentary behavior, dietary patterns, and environmental influences specific to the endomorph body type. Lifestyle modifications guided by endomorph-specific considerations aim to optimize diabetes management outcomes.

Advancements in Non-Invasive Monitoring for Endomorphs:

The quest for non-invasive monitoring methods for diabetes in endomorphs is an area of ongoing research. Future developments may include innovations in non-invasive glucose monitoring technologies, such as optical sensors, skin patches, and wearable devices tailored to the physiological characteristics of endomorphs. These advancements aim to offer more comfortable and user-friendly monitoring solutions.

Incorporating Endomorph Considerations in Diabetes Education:

Ensuring that diabetes education programs are tailored to the needs of endomorphs is an essential aspect of ongoing research. Future developments may involve the integration of endomorph-specific considerations into educational materials, self-management resources, and support initiatives. Empowering individuals with the endomorph body type with targeted knowledge enhances their ability to navigate diabetes management effectively.

Collaborative Research on Endomorph-Related Complications:

Research on diabetes-related complications specific to endomorphs is a critical area of focus. Future developments may involve collaborative efforts to understand the risk factors, prevalence, and management strategies for complications such as cardiovascular issues, neuropathy, and kidney disease in individuals with the endomorph body type. This knowledge informs comprehensive care approaches.

Patient-Reported Outcomes and Endomorph-Specific Quality of Life:

Assessing patient-reported outcomes and understanding the quality of life specific to endomorphs with diabetes is an emerging research domain. Future developments may involve studies that explore the impact of diabetes on daily life, emotional well-being, and social functioning in individuals with the endomorph body type. Insights from these studies can guide holistic and patient-centered care.

Ethical Considerations in Endomorph-Specific Research:

As research endeavors focus on endomorph-specific aspects of diabetes management, ethical considerations become paramount. Future developments may involve guidelines and frameworks for conducting ethical research that respects the rights, privacy, and dignity of individuals with the endomorph body type. Ensuring inclusivity and cultural sensitivity in research practices is an ongoing priority.

In conclusion, research and developments specific to endomorphs with diabetes are expanding our understanding of the intricate interplay between genetics, metabolism, and lifestyle factors. As these initiatives progress, they hold the potential to reshape diabetes care, providing more targeted and effective interventions tailored to the unique characteristics and challenges associated with the endomorph body type.

Conclusion

In the journey of living with diabetes as an endomorph, the path is paved with unique challenges and considerations. As we conclude this comprehensive exploration, it is crucial to focus on empowering endomorphs to not just manage their diabetes but to truly live well with it. This concluding section delves into the importance of empowerment, the role of education, building a resilient mindset, and fostering a sense of community to support individuals with the endomorph body type in their diabetes management journey.

Understanding the Power of Empowerment:

Empowerment is a powerful tool in the realm of diabetes management, especially for individuals with the endomorph body type. Empowering endomorphs involves providing them with the knowledge, skills, and confidence to actively participate in their diabetes care. It goes beyond the traditional patient-provider dynamic, emphasizing a collaborative approach where individuals feel in control of their health decisions and outcomes.

Empowerment in the context of diabetes includes understanding one's body, being proficient in monitoring and managing blood glucose levels, making informed lifestyle choices, and actively engaging in shared decision-making with healthcare providers. For endomorphs, who may face additional challenges related to metabolism and weight management, empowerment becomes a crucial aspect of navigating the complexities of diabetes while embracing their unique body type.

Education as a Catalyst for Empowerment:

Education catalyzes empowerment, equipping endomorphs with the knowledge and understanding needed to make informed decisions about their diabetes care. It begins with a comprehensive understanding of diabetes itself—its types, causes, symptoms, and treatment options. Specific education tailored to the endomorph body type encompasses insights into metabolic characteristics, genetic predispositions, and lifestyle considerations.

Education extends to practical skills such as meal planning, understanding medication regimens, interpreting blood glucose readings, and incorporating physical activity into daily life. For endomorphs, understanding how their body type influences these aspects is key to making sustainable and effective choices. Diabetes education fosters a sense of self-efficacy, enabling individuals to actively engage in their care with confidence.

Building a Resilient Mindset:

Living well with diabetes as an endomorph requires not just physical resilience but also a resilient mindset. The emotional and psychological aspects of diabetes management are integral to overall well-being. Building resilience involves developing the ability to adapt to challenges, bounce back from setbacks, and maintain a positive outlook in the face of adversity.

For endomorphs, who may contend with weight-related concerns and metabolic intricacies, resilience becomes a cornerstone of navigating the emotional complexities of diabetes. It involves recognizing that diabetes management is a continuous journey with ups and downs, and setbacks are not indicators of failure but opportunities for learning and growth.

Mindfulness practices, stress management techniques, and seeking support from mental health professionals contribute to building a resilient mindset. Embracing a proactive approach to emotional well-being empowers endomorphs to face the emotional challenges of diabetes with strength and optimism, fostering a holistic sense of resilience.

Community Support and Shared Experiences:

No one should navigate the path of diabetes alone, and this rings especially true for individuals with the endomorph body type. Building a sense of community support involves connecting with others who share similar experiences, challenges, and triumphs. Whether through local support groups, online forums, or community events, the power of shared experiences cannot be overstated.

The sense of community provides a platform for individuals to exchange practical tips, emotional support, and encouragement. It breaks the isolation that can sometimes accompany living with a chronic condition. For endomorphs, sharing insights into managing diabetes within the context of their body type creates a supportive environment where individuals feel understood and valued.

Online platforms and social media groups dedicated to endomorphs with diabetes facilitate the exchange of information and experiences on a global scale. Virtual connections offer a sense of camaraderie and a reminder that individuals are not alone in their journey. Building a supportive community is a cornerstone of empowering endomorphs to live well with diabetes.

Tailoring Lifestyle Choices to Individual Preferences:

Empowering endomorphs involves recognizing the diversity of lifestyle choices and tailoring recommendations to individual preferences. While general guidelines for nutrition, exercise, and stress management exist, the key is to work with individuals to find strategies that resonate with their unique preferences, cultural backgrounds, and daily routines.

For nutrition, this may involve exploring diverse dietary patterns and finding a balance that aligns with individual tastes while meeting diabetes management goals. Tailored exercise routines take into account personal interests and physical abilities, ensuring that physical activity is enjoyable and sustainable. Stress management strategies are individualized, recognizing that different approaches resonate with different people.

By acknowledging and respecting individual preferences, empowerment becomes a personalized journey. This approach fosters a sense of ownership over lifestyle choices, making it more likely that individuals will adhere to and derive satisfaction from their chosen strategies. Empowering endomorphs involves recognizing the importance of individuality in diabetes management.

Encouraging Regular Monitoring and Health Check-Ups:

Empowerment also involves a proactive approach to health monitoring and regular check-ups. Encouraging endomorphs to regularly monitor their blood glucose levels provides valuable insights into how lifestyle choices impact their diabetes management. It allows for timely adjustments to medication regimens, dietary plans, and exercise routines based on real-time data.

Regular health check-ups, including screenings for diabetes-related complications, are integral to preventive care. For endomorphs, who may have specific considerations related to metabolism and weight management, proactive monitoring becomes even more crucial. It allows healthcare providers to identify and address potential issues early, optimizing long-term health outcomes.

Empowering endomorphs to take an active role in their health monitoring fosters a sense of agency and accountability. It encourages a partnership between individuals and healthcare providers, working together to achieve optimal diabetes management outcomes. Regular monitoring and check-ups serve as proactive measures in the journey to live well with diabetes.

Promoting a Positive Body Image and Self-Care:

The intersection of body image and diabetes management is a significant aspect of empowerment for endomorphs. Promoting a positive body image involves recognizing and appreciating the body for its resilience, strength, and uniqueness. It emphasizes that the value of an individual goes beyond physical appearance and is not defined by the presence of diabetes.

Self-care practices play a crucial role in promoting a positive body image. This includes prioritizing adequate sleep, engaging in enjoyable physical activities, and incorporating stress-reducing activities into daily life. For endomorphs, self-care involves embracing the body as it is, recognizing that it can thrive and achieve optimal health despite the complexities of diabetes.

Cultivating a positive body image contributes to mental and emotional well-being, fostering a sense of self-love and acceptance. It aligns with the concept of holistic health, recognizing that well-being encompasses physical, mental, and emotional dimensions. Empowering endomorphs involves promoting self-care practices that contribute to a positive and nurturing relationship with their bodies.

Advocacy for Inclusivity and Accessibility:

Empowerment extends beyond individual well-being to advocating for inclusivity and accessibility within the broader healthcare system. For endomorphs, who may encounter specific challenges related to body size and metabolic factors, advocating for a healthcare environment that is inclusive, understanding, and free from judgment becomes an important aspect of empowerment.

Inclusivity in healthcare involves recognizing and addressing biases, stereotypes, and stigmas associated with body size. It advocates for healthcare professionals who approach diabetes management with cultural competence, recognizing the unique needs of individuals with the endomorph body type. It also involves promoting research, education, and awareness campaigns that embrace diversity in body sizes and shapes.

Accessibility in healthcare ensures that individuals, regardless of their body type, have equitable access to diabetes care, education, and support. This includes addressing barriers such as financial constraints, geographical disparities, and cultural considerations. Advocacy for inclusivity and accessibility aligns with the principles of empowerment, ensuring that all individuals can access the resources and support needed to live well with diabetes.

Celebrating Achievements and Milestones:

As we conclude the journey of exploring diabetes management for endomorphs, it is essential to celebrate achievements and milestones along the way. Recognizing progress, both big and small, contributes to a positive mindset and reinforces the sense of empowerment. Celebrations serve as reminders that living well with diabetes is not only an ongoing journey but also a series of victories and accomplishments.

Achievements may include reaching and maintaining target blood glucose levels, adopting and sustaining healthy lifestyle habits, overcoming specific challenges, and contributing to the diabetes community. Celebrating achievements creates a culture of positivity and resilience, motivating individuals to continue their efforts in diabetes management.

For endomorphs, celebrating achievements also involves acknowledging the unique aspects of their diabetes journey. Whether it's achieving weight-related goals, optimizing metabolic health, or mastering personalized lifestyle strategies, each milestone is a testament to resilience and dedication. Empowerment is fueled by the recognition that every step forward is a triumph worth celebrating.

Empowering endomorphs to live well with diabetes is a multifaceted and ongoing process. It involves education, resilience, community support, personalized strategies, proactive health monitoring, positive body image, advocacy, and the celebration of achievements. By fostering empowerment, individuals with the endomorph body type can navigate their diabetes journey with confidence, actively participating in their care and achieving holistic well-being. The path to living well with diabetes is not without challenges, but with empowerment, it becomes a journey of strength, resilience, and meaningful accomplishments.

Appendix A: Recipe Ideas for Endomorphs

Living with diabetes as an endomorph involves making mindful choices when it comes to nutrition. Maintaining a balanced and nutrient-rich diet is crucial for managing blood sugar levels and promoting overall health. This collection of recipe ideas is tailored to the specific needs and preferences of individuals with the endomorph body type. These recipes focus on incorporating wholesome ingredients, portion control, and flavors that cater to a diverse palate.

1. **Quinoa and Vegetable Stir-Fry:**
   - Ingredients:
     - 1 cup quinoa (cooked)
     - Mixed vegetables (broccoli, bell peppers, carrots)
     - Tofu or lean chicken strips
     - Low-sodium soy sauce
     - Garlic and ginger for flavor
   - Instructions:

     - In a pan, stir-fry tofu or chicken with garlic and ginger.
     - Add a variety of colorful vegetables and continue cooking until tender.
     - Mix in cooked quinoa and drizzle with low-sodium soy sauce.

- Toss the ingredients until well combined, creating a flavorful and nutrient-packed stir-fry.

2. **Salmon and Avocado Salad:**

- Ingredients:

    - Grilled or baked salmon fillet

    - Mixed salad greens (spinach, arugula, and kale)

    - Cherry tomatoes, sliced cucumber, and radishes

    - Avocado slices

    - Olive oil and lemon dressing

- Instructions:

    - Grill or bake salmon until fully cooked.
    - In a bowl, combine mixed salad greens, cherry tomatoes, cucumber, radishes, and avocado slices.
    - Top the salad with the cooked salmon.
    - Drizzle with a light dressing made from olive oil and freshly squeezed lemon juice.

3. **Sweet Potato and Chickpea Curry:**

- Ingredients:

    - Sweet potatoes, peeled and diced

    - Chickpeas (canned or cooked)

    - Onion, garlic, and ginger

    - Coconut milk

- Curry powder, cumin, and coriander for seasoning
- Instructions:
  - Sauté onions, garlic, and ginger in a pot until fragrant.
  - Add diced sweet potatoes and chickpeas to the pot.
  - Season with curry powder, cumin, and coriander.
  - Pour in coconut milk and simmer until sweet potatoes are tender.
  - Serve the curry over brown rice or quinoa.

4. **Turkey and Vegetable Skewers:**
   - Ingredients:
     - Lean ground turkey
     - Colorful bell peppers, cherry tomatoes, and red onion
     - Olive oil and herbs for marinating
   - Instructions:
     - Mix ground turkey with olive oil and your choice of herbs for marination.
     - Thread ground turkey and colorful vegetables onto skewers.
     - Grill or bake until the turkey is fully cooked and the vegetables are tender.

- Serve the skewers with a side of Greek yogurt and fresh herbs.

5. **Mushroom and Spinach Omelette:**

   - Ingredients:

     - Eggs

     - Mushrooms, sliced

     - Fresh spinach leaves

     - Cherry tomatoes, halved

     - Feta cheese (optional)

   - Instructions:

     - Whisk eggs in a bowl and pour into a heated non-stick pan.

     - Add sliced mushrooms, fresh spinach leaves, and cherry tomatoes.

     - Cook until the eggs are set, and the vegetables are tender.

     - Optional: Sprinkle with feta cheese for added flavor.

6. **Greek Yogurt Parfait with Berries:**

   - Ingredients:

     - Greek yogurt (unsweetened)

     - Mixed berries (blueberries, strawberries, raspberries)

     - Granola (low-sugar or homemade)

     - Drizzle of honey

- Instructions:

    - In a glass or bowl, layer Greek yogurt with mixed berries.

    - Sprinkle granola on top for added crunch.

    - Drizzle with a touch of honey for sweetness.

7. **Vegetable and Lentil Soup:**

   - Ingredients:

       - Brown lentils (cooked)

       - Mixed vegetables (carrots, celery, zucchini)

       - Low-sodium vegetable broth

       - Garlic, onion, and thyme for seasoning

   - Instructions:

       - Sauté garlic and onion in a pot until softened.

       - Add mixed vegetables and cooked brown lentils.

       - Pour in low-sodium vegetable broth and season with thyme.

       - Simmer until the vegetables are tender, creating a hearty and nutritious soup.

These recipe ideas offer a starting point for crafting delicious and diabetes-friendly meals tailored to the endomorph body type. It's essential to personalize these recipes based on individual preferences, dietary restrictions, and nutritional needs. Experimenting with diverse flavors and incorporating a variety of nutrient-dense foods can contribute to a satisfying and well-balanced diet for individuals living with diabetes as endomorphs.

Appendix B: Sample Workout Plans

Staying physically active is a crucial aspect of managing diabetes for individuals with the endomorph body type. Regular exercise not only helps improve insulin sensitivity but also supports overall health and well-being. These sample workout plans are designed with the specific needs of endomorphs in mind, considering factors such as metabolism, weight management, and cardiovascular health. It's important to consult with a healthcare professional before starting any new exercise regimen.

Workout Plan 1: Cardiovascular Focus
Duration: 30 minutes

1. **Warm-up (5 minutes):**

   - Light cardio exercises such as brisk walking or cycling to increase heart rate and warm up muscles.

2. **Cardiovascular Exercise (20 minutes):**

   - Choose activities like brisk walking, jogging, or cycling.

   - Include intervals of increased intensity to elevate heart rate.

   - Aim for a mix of moderate and vigorous intensity throughout the session.

3. **Strength Training (5 minutes):**

   - Bodyweight exercises such as squats, lunges, and push-ups.

   - Focus on controlled movements and proper form.

   - Perform 2 sets of 10-15 repetitions for each exercise.

4. **Cool Down and Stretching (5 minutes):**

- Gentle stretching for major muscle groups to improve flexibility.

- Include stretches for calves, quadriceps, hamstrings, and upper body.

Workout Plan 2: Interval Training for Metabolism Boost

Duration: 40 minutes

1. **Warm-up (7 minutes):**

   - Jumping jacks, high knees, or dynamic stretching to prepare the body for exercise.

2. **Interval Cardio Training (25 minutes):**

   - Alternate between periods of high-intensity exercises (e.g., sprinting or jumping) and periods of lower intensity (e.g., walking or light jogging).

   - Include both cardiovascular and strength-based exercises.

   - Aim for 30 seconds of high intensity followed by 30 seconds of lower intensity.

3. **Strength Training Circuit (10 minutes):**

   - Full-body strength exercises using resistance bands or dumbbells.

   - Perform a circuit of exercises with minimal rest between sets.

   - Include squats, lunges, bicep curls, and shoulder presses.

4. **Cool Down and Stretch (8 minutes):**

   - Gentle yoga or static stretches to improve flexibility and prevent muscle tightness.

- Focus on breathing and relaxation during the cool-down.

Workout Plan 3: Low-Impact Exercise Routine

Duration: 45 minutes

1. **Low-Impact Cardio (20 minutes):**

   - Walking or marching in place.

   - Low-impact aerobic exercises like side steps and knee lifts to avoid excessive stress on joints.

2. **Strength and Stability (15 minutes):**

   - Bodyweight exercises emphasizing stability and balance.

   - Include exercises such as planks, leg raises, and wall sits.

   - Perform 2 sets of 12-15 repetitions for each exercise.

3. **Light Cardio and Aerobics (10 minutes):**

   - Incorporate light aerobic exercises like dancing or low-impact aerobics.

   - Focus on enjoyment and maintaining a steady pace.

4. **Flexibility and Relaxation (5 minutes):**

   - Gentle stretching exercises to enhance flexibility.

   - Include deep breathing or meditation to promote relaxation.

Workout Plan 4: Endurance and Long Walks

Duration: 60 minutes

1. **Brisk Walking (45 minutes):**

- Engage in brisk walking, maintaining a steady pace.

- Choose scenic routes or nature trails for added enjoyment.

2. **Interval Training (10 minutes):**

- Incorporate short bursts of faster walking or light jogging.

- Gradually increase the intensity during intervals.

3. **Strength Training (5 minutes):**

- Include bodyweight exercises like squats, lunges, and push-ups.

- Focus on maintaining proper form and controlled movements.

4. **Cool Down and Stretching (10 minutes):**

- Gentle stretching for major muscle groups.

- Incorporate dynamic stretches and focus on breathing during the cool-down.

Important Notes:

- Always start with a warm-up to prepare your body for exercise.

- Stay hydrated throughout the workout.

- Listen to your body and modify exercises as needed.

- If you have any health concerns or conditions, consult with your healthcare provider before beginning a new exercise program.

- Gradually progress the intensity and duration of your workouts to avoid overexertion.

Remember, consistency is key when it comes to exercise. Choose activities that you enjoy, and make adjustments based on your fitness level and preferences. Regular physical activity not only contributes to better diabetes management but also promotes overall health and vitality for individuals with the endomorph body type

Glossary

1. Diabetes:

- A chronic medical condition characterized by elevated levels of blood glucose (sugar). There are different types of diabetes, including Type 1, Type 2, and gestational diabetes.

2. Endomorph:

- One of the three basic somatotypes, referring to individuals with a naturally higher percentage of body fat, a rounder physique, and a slower metabolism.

3. Insulin:

- A hormone produced by the pancreas that regulates blood sugar by facilitating the absorption of glucose into cells for energy.

4. Blood Glucose:

- The concentration of glucose (sugar) present in the bloodstream. It is a key indicator of diabetes management.

5. Metabolism:

- The process by which the body converts food and beverages into energy. The metabolic rate varies among individuals and can impact weight management.

6. Body Mass Index (BMI):

- A numerical measure of body fat based on height and weight. It is often used to categorize individuals into different weight status categories.

7. Cardiovascular Exercise:

- Physical activities that elevate the heart rate and improve cardiovascular health. Examples include walking, jogging, cycling, and swimming.

8. Strength Training:

- Exercises designed to build and strengthen muscles. This can include weightlifting, resistance training, and bodyweight exercises.

9. Insulin Resistance:

- A condition where the body's cells become less responsive to the effects of insulin, leading to elevated blood glucose levels.

10. Glycemic Index (GI):

- A measure of how quickly a carbohydrate-containing food raises blood glucose levels. Foods with a high GI are rapidly digested and cause a quicker spike in blood sugar.

11. Nutrient-Rich:

- Foods that provide a high concentration of essential nutrients relative to their calorie content. Nutrient-dense foods are important for overall health and diabetes management.

12. Continuous Glucose Monitoring (CGM):

- A technology that tracks glucose levels throughout the day and night. It involves a small sensor placed under the skin, providing real-time data to help manage diabetes.

13. Body Image:

- A person's perception and attitude towards their own body. Positive body image involves accepting and appreciating one's body for its unique qualities.

14. Resilience:

- The ability to adapt and bounce back from challenges or setbacks. Resilience is crucial for emotional well-being, especially in the context of managing chronic conditions like diabetes.

15. Somatotype:

- A categorization of body types based on physical characteristics. The three primary somatotypes are endomorph, mesomorph, and ectomorph.

16. Interval Training:

- A type of cardiovascular exercise that alternates between short bursts of intense activity and periods of lower-intensity or rest.

17. Flexibility:

- The range of motion in joints and muscles. Flexibility exercises, such as stretching, contribute to overall physical health.

18. Inclusivity:

- Creating an environment that embraces and respects diversity, ensuring that all individuals, regardless of body type or other factors, feel included.

19. Empowerment:

- The process of enabling individuals to take control of their lives, make informed decisions, and actively participate in their health and well-being.

20. Advocacy:

- The act of supporting and speaking up for the rights and needs of a particular group. In the context of diabetes, advocacy may involve promoting inclusivity, awareness, and access to resources.

PROSTATE CANCER PATIENTS FOR NEWLY DIAGNOSED: A
Comprehensive Guide to Diagnosis, Treatment, and Recovery

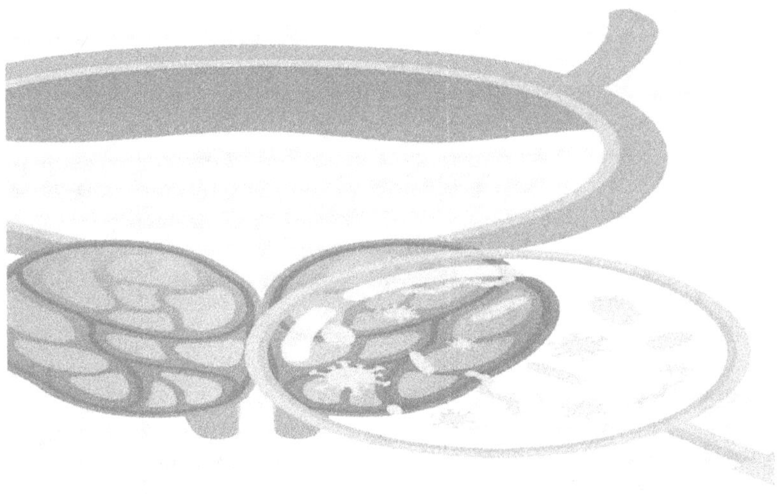

ETHEL D. AYE

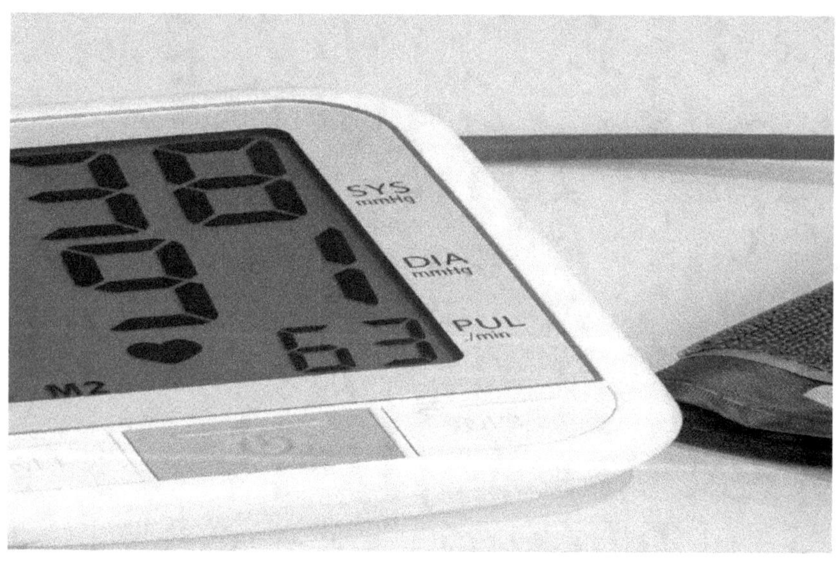

INTRODUCTION

A Journey with Prostate Cancer"
In the quiet moments following his diagnosis of prostate cancer, John found himself engulfed in a whirlwind of emotions - fear, uncertainty, and a profound sense of vulnerability.

Sitting in the sterile confines of the doctor's office, the weight of his diagnosis pressed heavily upon him, casting a shadow over his once-secure world. With a trembling hand, he accepted the doctor's words, feeling as though his life had suddenly been thrown into disarray.

As John grappled with the reality of his diagnosis, he found solace in the supportive embrace of his loved ones. His wife, Susan, stood by his side with unwavering strength and compassion, offering a steady hand to hold amidst the storm.

Together, they embarked on a journey of discovery, seeking out answers, guidance, and hope in the face of uncertainty.
Amidst the chaos of doctor's appointments and treatment discussions, John stumbled upon a book that would change the course of his journey.

Tucked away on a dusty shelf in the corner of the bookstore, its title spoke directly to his heart: " **Prostate Cancer patients for newly diagnosed:** A Comprehensive Guide to Diagnosis, Treatment, and Recovery."

With trembling hands, John turned the pages of the book, devouring its contents with an insatiable hunger for knowledge and understanding. Within its pages, he found a wealth of information, guidance, and practical advice to navigate the complexities of his diagnosis and treatment options.

As he delved deeper into the book's pages, John felt a newfound sense of empowerment and hope begin to bloom within him. Armed with knowledge and supported by the love of his family, he embarked on his journey with renewed courage and determination.

With each passing day, John drew strength from the wisdom imparted by the book, embracing its teachings as a beacon of light amidst the darkness of his diagnosis. Through its guidance, he found the courage to face his fears, the resilience to endure the challenges ahead, and the hope to believe in a future beyond cancer.

As John's journey unfolded, he discovered that healing was not simply a destination to be reached but a journey to be embraced - a journey of courage, resilience, and unwavering determination in the face of adversity. And with each step forward, he found himself drawing ever closer to the healing he so desperately sought.

CHAPTER 1:

UNDERSTANDING PROSTATE CANCER

Understanding Prostate Cancer for those newly diagnosed involves gaining insights into the intricacies of this condition, empowering individuals with the knowledge necessary to navigate the journey ahead.

Prostate cancer begins in the small, walnut-shaped gland known as the prostate, located below the bladder and surrounding the urethra. Its primary function is to produce seminal fluid, aiding in the transportation of sperm. When cells in the prostate undergo abnormal growth, they can form tumors, leading to prostate cancer.

One crucial aspect of comprehension is recognizing the various risk factors associated with prostate cancer. Age plays a significant role, with the likelihood of developing prostate cancer increasing as men grow older.

Family history, genetics, and race also contribute to the risk profile, underlining the importance of understanding one's individual risk factors. While the exact cause of prostate cancer remains elusive, lifestyle factors such as diet, exercise, and exposure to certain environmental elements may influence its development.

For those newly diagnosed, understanding the stages and types of prostate cancer is essential. The stages range from localized (confined to the prostate) to advanced (spread beyond the prostate), guiding treatment decisions. Additionally, prostate cancers can be classified as either slow-growing (low-grade) or aggressive (high-grade), influencing the urgency and intensity of interventions.

Importance of Early Detection

Early detection of prostate cancer is paramount in ensuring successful treatment outcomes and improving the overall prognosis for newly diagnosed patients.

Prostate cancer is the second most common cancer among men worldwide, and its incidence tends to increase with age.

Detecting the disease in its early stages offers several critical advantages.

Firstly, early detection allows for more effective and less invasive treatment options. When prostate cancer is identified at an early stage, interventions such as surgery, radiation therapy, or targeted therapies are more likely to be successful.

This can significantly reduce the impact of the disease on a patient's life and increase the chances of a full recovery.
Secondly, early detection enables healthcare professionals to tailor treatment plans based on the specific characteristics of the cancer.

Not all prostate cancers behave the same way, and personalized approaches can be developed when the disease is caught early. This ensures that patients receive the most appropriate and targeted interventions, minimizing unnecessary side effects and complications.

Moreover, early detection can lead to a better quality of life for prostate cancer patients. Timely identification allows for prompt management of symptoms and potential side effects, contributing to a more comfortable and manageable treatment experience. It also provides an opportunity for patients to engage in supportive care and make informed decisions about their health.

Regular screenings and check-ups play a crucial role in early detection, especially for individuals with risk factors such as age, family history, or certain genetic predispositions.

Encouraging awareness and proactive health-seeking behavior can empower individuals to take charge of their well-being and catch potential issues before they escalate.

CHAPTER 2: BASICS OF PROSTATE CANCER

Anatomy and Function of the Prostate

The prostate is a small, walnut-shaped gland that plays a crucial role in the male reproductive system. Situated just below the bladder and in front of the rectum, the prostate surrounds the urethra, the tube that carries urine and semen out of the body. Understanding the anatomy and function of the prostate is essential for newly diagnosed prostate cancer patients.

The primary function of the prostate is to produce a fluid that nourishes and transports sperm during ejaculation. This prostatic fluid, rich in enzymes and nutrients, constitutes a significant portion of semen. The muscles of the prostate also aid in propelling the seminal fluid into the urethra during ejaculation.

Prostate cancer occurs when abnormal cells within the prostate start to multiply uncontrollably, forming a tumor. As the tumor grows, it can interfere with the normal function of the prostate and may eventually spread to other parts of the body.

The proximity of the prostate to the urethra can lead to urinary symptoms in prostate cancer patients. These may include difficulty in urination, frequent urination, weak urine flow, or a feeling of incomplete emptying of the bladder. Understanding these potential symptoms is crucial for patients and healthcare providers in identifying and diagnosing prostate cancer at an early stage. Moreover, the anatomy of the prostate influences the treatment options available for prostate cancer. Surgical interventions, such as radical prostatectomy, involve the removal of the entire prostate gland. Radiation therapy may also be employed to target and destroy cancerous cells within the prostate.

What is Prostate Cancer?

Prostate cancer is a form of cancer that develops in the prostate, a small, walnut-sized gland located just below the bladder and in front of the rectum in men. The prostate plays a crucial role in the male reproductive system, producing seminal fluid that nourishes and transports sperm during ejaculation.

Prostate cancer occurs when cells in the prostate undergo abnormal changes and begin to proliferate uncontrollably, forming a tumor. This tumor can vary in its nature, ranging from slow-growing and non-aggressive to fast-growing and potentially spreading to other parts of the body.

The exact cause of prostate cancer is not fully understood, but certain risk factors have been identified. Age is a significant factor, with the risk of prostate cancer increasing with age. Family history, genetic predisposition, and race also play a role, as men of African descent have a higher incidence of prostate cancer.

Early stages of prostate cancer often present with no noticeable symptoms, making regular screenings and check-ups critical for early detection. As the disease progresses, some men may experience symptoms such as difficulty urinating, frequent urination, blood in the urine or semen, and discomfort in the pelvic area. However, these symptoms are not exclusive to prostate cancer and may also be associated with other conditions.

Diagnosis typically involves a combination of a digital rectal exam (DRE), measuring prostate-specific antigen (PSA) levels in the blood, and imaging studies. Biopsy, where a small sample of prostate tissue is taken for examination, is often performed to confirm the presence of cancer and determine its characteristics.

Treatment options for prostate cancer depend on factors such as the stage of the cancer, the aggressiveness of the tumor, and the overall health of the patient. Common approaches include surgery, radiation therapy, hormone therapy, and watchful waiting or active surveillance.

Prostate cancer awareness, regular screenings, and prompt medical attention are crucial in managing and treating this prevalent cancer, ultimately improving outcomes and preserving the overall well-being of affected individuals

Causes and Risk Factors

The causes of prostate cancer are not fully understood, but several risk factors have been identified that may increase an individual's likelihood of developing this condition. Understanding these factors is crucial for newly diagnosed prostate cancer patients and their healthcare providers.

Age is a significant risk factor, with the incidence of prostate cancer increasing with age. The majority of cases are diagnosed in men over the age of 65.

Family history also plays a role, as individuals with close relatives, such as a father or brother, who have had prostate cancer are at a higher risk. Genetic factors further contribute to susceptibility, with certain gene mutations and inherited conditions potentially increasing the likelihood of developing prostate cancer.

Race and ethnicity are additional risk factors, as prostate cancer is more common in African-American men and less common in Asian and Hispanic men. The reasons for these racial disparities are not entirely clear but may involve a combination of genetic, environmental, and healthcare access factors.

Lifestyle and dietary choices have also been linked to prostate cancer risk. Diets high in red and processed meats, low in fruits and vegetables, and high in fat have been associated with an increased risk of developing prostate cancer. Additionally, obesity and a sedentary lifestyle may contribute to the likelihood of developing more aggressive forms of the disease.

Environmental factors, such as exposure to certain chemicals or toxins, may also play a role in prostate cancer development. However, the specific associations between environmental factors and prostate cancer risk are still an area of ongoing research.

For newly diagnosed prostate cancer patients, understanding these causes and risk factors can guide discussions with healthcare providers, inform treatment decisions, and contribute to proactive lifestyle changes that may help manage the disease and improve overall outcomes.

Regular screenings, especially for individuals with multiple risk factors, become essential in early detection and effective management of prostate cancer.

Types and Stages of Prostate Cancer

Prostate cancer is a heterogeneous disease, meaning it can manifest in various forms, each with different characteristics and behaviors. Understanding the types and stages of prostate cancer is crucial for newly diagnosed patients and their healthcare teams.

The two main types of prostate cancer are adenocarcinoma and neuroendocrine tumors. Adenocarcinoma is the most common type, originating from the glandular cells of the prostate. Neuroendocrine tumors are less common but tend to be more aggressive. Differentiating between these types is essential for determining the appropriate treatment approach.

Prostate cancer is staged based on the extent of its spread, and the most widely used staging system is the TNM system (Tumor, Node, Metastasis). The T stage evaluates the size and extent of the primary tumor, the N stage assesses the involvement of nearby lymph nodes, and the M stage indicates whether the cancer has metastasized to distant organs.

The stages range from I to IV, with subcategories providing more detailed information. In Stage I, the cancer is confined to the prostate and is often slow-growing. Stage II involves a larger tumor but is still localized within the prostate.

Stage III signifies the cancer has spread beyond the prostate but is limited to nearby tissues. Stage IV indicates advanced cancer with potential spread to distant organs, such as bones or lymph nodes. Understanding the stage is crucial for treatment decisions and prognosis. Early-stage prostate cancer (I and II) may be managed with localized treatments like surgery or radiation therapy. Advanced stages (III and IV) may require more comprehensive approaches, including hormone therapy, chemotherapy, or immunotherapy.

For newly diagnosed prostate cancer patients, the knowledge of the specific type and stage of their cancer is instrumental in developing a personalized treatment plan.

It allows for informed decision-making, tailored interventions, and a comprehensive approach to managing the disease throughout its various stages. Regular monitoring and collaboration with healthcare professionals ensure that the chosen treatment strategies align with the evolving nature of the cancer.

CHAPTER 3: DIAGNOSIS

Signs and Symptoms

Receiving a diagnosis of prostate cancer can be overwhelming, but understanding the signs and symptoms can empower patients to take control of their health journey.

While prostate cancer may initially present with no noticeable symptoms in its early stages, as the disease progresses, certain signs may become apparent. Here are some common signs and symptoms newly diagnosed prostate cancer patients should be aware of:

Urinary Changes: Changes in urinary habits can be one of the earliest signs of prostate cancer. Patients may experience increased frequency of urination, especially at night (nocturia). They may also notice a weak or interrupted urine flow, difficulty starting or stopping urination, or a sense of incomplete emptying of the bladder.

Blood in Urine or Semen: Hematuria (blood in urine) or hematospermia (blood in semen) can occur in some cases of prostate cancer. While these symptoms can be alarming, they are not always indicative of cancer and can have other causes as well. Nevertheless, they warrant prompt medical evaluation.

Erectile Dysfunction: Prostate cancer can impact erectile function due to its proximity to the nerves and blood vessels responsible for erections. Erectile dysfunction may occur as a result of the cancer itself or due to treatments such as surgery or radiation therapy.
Pelvic Pain: Some men with prostate cancer may experience discomfort or pain in the pelvic area, lower back, hips, or thighs. This pain can vary in intensity and may be persistent or intermittent.

Bone Pain: Advanced prostate cancer may spread to the bones, leading to bone pain, especially in the spine, hips, and pelvis. Bone pain may worsen at night and with movement.
Unintended Weight Loss:

Significant and unexplained weight loss can be a sign of advanced prostate cancer. Cancer-related weight loss often occurs due to a combination of factors, including decreased appetite, metabolic changes, and the body's response to the disease.

Screening and Diagnostic Tests

For newly diagnosed prostate cancer patients, understanding the screening and diagnostic tests available is crucial for determining the extent of the disease and developing an appropriate treatment plan. Here are some key screening and diagnostic tests commonly used in the evaluation of prostate cancer:

Digital Rectal Exam (DRE): During a digital rectal exam, a healthcare provider inserts a lubricated, gloved finger into the rectum to feel the prostate gland for any abnormalities, such as lumps or enlargement.

While DRE alone cannot diagnose prostate cancer definitively, it can provide valuable information about the size, shape, and texture of the prostate. Prostate-Specific Antigen (PSA) Test: The PSA test measures the level of prostate-specific antigen, a protein produced by the prostate gland, in the blood.

Elevated PSA levels can indicate the presence of prostate cancer, though other factors such as age, prostate size, and inflammation can also affect

PSA levels. A high PSA level may prompt further diagnostic testing.

Prostate Biopsy: A prostate biopsy is the most definitive diagnostic test for prostate cancer. During this procedure, a urologist collects small samples of tissue from the prostate gland using a thin needle guided by ultrasound imaging.

These tissue samples are then examined under a microscope by a pathologist to determine if cancer cells are present and to assess the grade and stage of the cancer.

Imaging Studies: Imaging studies such as transrectal ultrasound (TRUS), magnetic resonance imaging (MRI), computed tomography (CT) scans, and bone scans may be used to evaluate the extent of the cancer and detect any spread to nearby lymph nodes or distant organs, such as the bones.

These imaging tests help oncologists stage the cancer and determine the most appropriate treatment approach.

Genetic Testing: Genetic testing may be recommended for some prostate cancer patients, especially those with a family history of the disease or who are at high risk due to genetic mutations such as BRCA1 or BRCA2.

These tests can help identify inherited genetic mutations that may increase the risk of developing prostate cancer or influence treatment decisions.

Confirmatory Procedures (Biopsy, MRI, etc.)

Confirmatory procedures play a crucial role in providing a definitive diagnosis and guiding treatment decisions for newly diagnosed prostate cancer patients.

These procedures help oncologists accurately assess the extent and aggressiveness of the cancer, enabling personalized treatment plans tailored to each patient's specific needs. Here are some key confirmatory procedures commonly used in the management of prostate cancer:

> **Prostate Biopsy**: A prostate biopsy is often the initial confirmatory procedure following abnormal findings on screening tests such as the prostate-specific antigen (PSA) test or digital rectal exam (DRE).

During a biopsy, small samples of tissue are collected from the prostate gland using a thin needle guided by ultrasound imaging. These tissue samples are then examined under a microscope by a pathologist to determine if cancer cells are present and to assess the grade and stage of the cancer.

Biopsy results provide critical information for staging the cancer and determining the appropriate course of treatment.

> **Magnetic Resonance Imaging (MRI):** MRI imaging is increasingly used in the diagnosis and staging of prostate cancer.

Multiparametric MRI combines different MRI sequences to provide detailed images of the prostate gland and surrounding tissues. MRI can help detect and localize suspicious areas within the prostate, guide targeted biopsies to areas of concern, and assess the extent of the cancer, including whether it has spread beyond the prostate gland. MRI findings can aid in treatment planning and decision-making, particularly for patients considering active surveillance or focal therapy.

> **Computed Tomography (CT) Scan:** CT scans may be used to evaluate the extent of prostate cancer and detect any spread to

nearby lymph nodes or distant organs, such as the bones. While CT scans are less sensitive than MRI for imaging the prostate gland itself, they are valuable for staging purposes and determining the appropriate treatment approach, particularly for patients with advanced disease.

> **Bone Scan:** Bone scans are commonly performed to evaluate for the presence of prostate cancer metastases to the bones. This imaging test can detect areas of increased bone activity, known as "hot spots," which may indicate the presence of cancerous lesions. Bone scans are essential for staging the cancer and determining the extent of bone involvement, guiding treatment decisions and prognosis.

Understanding Prostate Specific Antigen (PSA) Levels

Understanding prostate-specific antigen (PSA) levels is essential for newly diagnosed prostate cancer patients as it provides valuable information about the presence and progression of the disease.

PSA is a protein produced by the prostate gland and released into the bloodstream.

While elevated PSA levels can indicate the presence of prostate cancer, they can also be influenced by other factors such as age, prostate size, inflammation, infection, and recent sexual activity. Here's what newly diagnosed prostate cancer patients need to know about PSA levels:

> **Normal PSA Levels:** In general, PSA levels below 4 nanograms per milliliter (ng/mL) are considered normal. However, PSA levels can vary among individuals, and what is considered normal may differ based on factors such as age, race, and overall prostate health. It's essential for patients to discuss their PSA levels with their healthcare provider to determine what is normal for them.

> **Elevated PSA Levels:** Elevated PSA levels above 4 ng/mL may indicate the presence of prostate cancer, but they can also result from other non-cancerous conditions such as benign prostatic hyperplasia (BPH), prostatitis (inflammation of the prostate), urinary tract infections, or recent prostate

procedures. In some cases, PSA levels may be elevated due to natural fluctuations or transient factors, requiring further evaluation to confirm the cause.

- ➢ **PSA Velocity and PSA Density:** In addition to absolute PSA levels, healthcare providers may assess PSA velocity (the rate of change in PSA levels over time) and PSA density (the ratio of PSA levels to prostate volume) to help determine the likelihood of prostate cancer and the need for further evaluation. Rapid increases in PSA levels or high PSA density may raise suspicion for prostate cancer and prompt additional testing such as a prostate biopsy.

- ➢ **Monitoring PSA Levels:** For newly diagnosed prostate cancer patients, regular monitoring of PSA levels is essential for assessing disease progression, monitoring response to treatment, and detecting potential recurrence. PSA testing may be performed at regular intervals following treatment to track PSA trends over time and detect any signs of disease recurrence or progression.

➢ **Interpreting PSA Results:** It's important for patients to understand that PSA testing is not a definitive diagnostic test for prostate cancer on its own. Elevated PSA levels may prompt further evaluation, including imaging studies and prostate biopsy, to confirm the presence of cancer and determine the appropriate course of treatment.

CHAPTER 4: TREATMENT OPTIONS

Active Surveillance

For newly diagnosed prostate cancer patients with low-risk or favorable intermediate-risk disease, active surveillance (AS) offers a conservative approach to managing their condition while minimizing the potential risks and side effects associated with immediate treatment.

AS involves regular monitoring of the cancer through a combination of PSA testing, digital rectal exams (DREs), and periodic imaging studies to track disease progression and detect any signs of advancement. Here's what newly diagnosed prostate cancer patients need to know about active surveillance:

> - **Patient Selection:** Active surveillance is typically recommended for patients with low-grade, low-volume prostate cancer that is confined to the prostate gland and has a low risk of progression or metastasis. Eligibility for active surveillance is determined based on various factors,

including PSA levels, Gleason score (a measure of prostate cancer aggressiveness), clinical stage, and tumor volume.

➢ **Monitoring Protocol:** Patients on active surveillance undergo regular monitoring, typically every 3 to 6 months initially, and less frequently as deemed appropriate by their healthcare provider. Monitoring includes PSA testing to track PSA levels over time, digital rectal exams to assess the size and consistency of the prostate gland, and periodic imaging studies such as MRI or ultrasound to evaluate any changes in the prostate or surrounding tissues.

➢ **Biopsy Surveillance:** Prostate biopsies may be performed periodically to assess disease progression and confirm the absence of aggressive features or higher-grade tumors. Repeat biopsies help oncologists evaluate changes in the cancer's characteristics over time and make informed decisions about the need for treatment.

➢ **Shared Decision-Making:** Choosing active surveillance requires active involvement and collaboration between patients and their healthcare providers. Patients should discuss the potential benefits and risks of active surveillance, including the possibility of disease progression and the need for eventual treatment, with their healthcare team to make an informed decision that aligns with their preferences and values.

➢ **Treatment Decision Points:** While active surveillance aims to defer treatment until necessary, patients on active surveillance may transition to active treatment if there are signs of disease progression or if they experience changes in their cancer characteristics that warrant intervention. Treatment options may include surgery, radiation therapy, or other targeted therapies depending on the individual's disease status and preferences.

Surgery (Prostatectomy)

Prostatectomy, the surgical removal of the prostate gland, is a common treatment option for prostate cancer patients, particularly those with localized disease or those who have failed other conservative treatments.

This procedure aims to remove the cancerous tissue while preserving urinary and sexual function to the extent possible. Here's an overview of prostatectomy:

> **Types of Prostatectomy:** There are several approaches to prostatectomy, including open surgery, laparoscopic surgery, robotic-assisted laparoscopic surgery (robotic prostatectomy), and nerve-sparing techniques. Open surgery involves a single large incision in the abdomen or perineum, while laparoscopic and robotic-assisted approaches use smaller incisions and specialized instruments for a minimally invasive procedure. Nerve-sparing techniques aim to preserve the nerves responsible for erectile function, reducing the risk of impotence following surgery.

> **Indications for Surgery:** Prostatectomy may be recommended for patients with localized prostate cancer that has not spread beyond the prostate gland and is deemed curable by surgical removal. It may also be recommended for patients with localized recurrence following other treatments such as radiation therapy or for those who are not

candidates for other treatments due to factors such as tumor size, location, or aggressiveness.

- ➢ **Preparation:** Prior to surgery, patients undergo a comprehensive evaluation, including imaging studies, blood tests, and possibly a prostate biopsy to confirm the diagnosis and assess the extent of the cancer. Patients may also undergo preoperative counseling to discuss the risks and benefits of surgery, as well as potential alternatives and postoperative expectations.

- ➢ **Procedure:** During prostatectomy, the surgeon removes the entire prostate gland along with nearby lymph nodes to reduce the risk of cancer recurrence. Depending on the surgical approach, the procedure may take several hours to complete. After removing the prostate, the surgeon reconstructs the urinary tract to restore urinary continence and, if possible, preserves the neurovascular bundles responsible for erectile function

- ➢ **Recovery and Follow-Up:** Following prostatectomy, patients typically stay in the hospital for a few days to recover and receive postoperative care. Recovery time varies depending on the surgical approach and individual factors but may take several weeks to months. Patients may experience temporary urinary incontinence and erectile dysfunction following surgery, though these side effects may improve over time with proper rehabilitation and support. Regular follow-up visits with the healthcare team are essential for monitoring recovery, assessing treatment effectiveness, and addressing any concerns or complications.

Radiation Therapy

Radiation therapy is a cornerstone treatment modality for prostate cancer, offering effective management of localized disease and providing an alternative to surgery for patients who may not be surgical candidates or prefer a non-invasive approach.

This treatment involves delivering high-energy radiation beams to the prostate gland and surrounding tissues to kill cancer cells and shrink tumors. Here's an overview of radiation therapy for prostate cancer:

➢ **Types of Radiation Therapy:** There are two main types of radiation therapy used in the treatment of prostate cancer: external beam radiation therapy (EBRT) and brachytherapy (internal radiation therapy). EBRT delivers radiation from outside the body using a machine called a linear accelerator, targeting the prostate gland and nearby tissues. Brachytherapy involves the implantation of radioactive seeds directly into the prostate gland, where they emit radiation to destroy cancer cells over time.

➢ **Indications for Radiation Therapy:** Radiation therapy may be recommended as a primary treatment for localized prostate cancer, particularly for patients with low to intermediate risk disease. It may also be used in combination with other treatments such as hormone therapy or as adjuvant therapy following surgery to reduce the risk of cancer recurrence. Additionally, radiation therapy may be used palliatively to relieve symptoms and improve quality of life in patients with advanced or metastatic prostate cancer.

➤ **Treatment Planning:** Prior to radiation therapy, patients undergo a comprehensive evaluation, including imaging studies and simulation sessions to precisely map the treatment area and determine the optimal radiation dose and delivery technique. Treatment planning aims to maximize the dose to the cancerous tissue while minimizing radiation exposure to nearby healthy organs and tissues, thereby reducing the risk of side effects.

➤ **Delivery and Administration:** Radiation therapy is typically administered over several weeks in daily sessions, with each treatment session lasting a few minutes. During treatment, patients lie on a treatment table while the radiation machine delivers targeted radiation beams to the prostate gland. Brachytherapy involves a one-time procedure to implant radioactive seeds directly into the prostate under ultrasound guidance.

➤ **Side Effects and Management:** Common side effects of radiation therapy for prostate cancer may include urinary symptoms such as frequency, urgency, and discomfort, as well as bowel irritation and fatigue. Most side effects are temporary and can be managed with supportive care, medications, and lifestyle modifications. Patients should communicate openly with their healthcare team about any side effects they experience to receive timely intervention and support.

Hormone Therapy

Hormone therapy, also known as androgen deprivation therapy (ADT), is a systemic treatment used in the management of prostate cancer, particularly for patients with advanced or metastatic disease. This therapy aims to suppress the production of male hormones, primarily testosterone, which fuels the growth and progression of prostate cancer cells.

By reducing testosterone levels, hormone therapy can slow down cancer growth, alleviate symptoms, and improve overall survival in prostate cancer patients. Here's an overview of hormone therapy for prostate cancer:

> **Mechanism of Action:** Prostate cancer cells rely on male hormones, particularly

testosterone, to grow and proliferate. Hormone therapy works by blocking the production of testosterone or inhibiting its action on cancer cells. This can be achieved through medications called luteinizing hormone-releasing hormone (LHRH) agonists or antagonists, which suppress the production of testosterone by the testes, or through anti-androgen medications, which block the action of testosterone on cancer cells.

➢ **Indications for Hormone Therapy:** Hormone therapy may be used in various settings for the treatment of prostate cancer, including as primary therapy for locally advanced or metastatic disease, in combination with radiation therapy for intermediate to high-risk localized disease, as adjuvant therapy following surgery or radiation to reduce the risk of recurrence, or as palliative therapy to relieve symptoms and improve quality of life in patients with advanced or metastatic disease.

➢ **Types of Hormone Therapy:** There are several types of hormone therapy used in the treatment of prostate cancer, including

LHRH agonists (e.g., leuprolide, goserelin), LHRH antagonists (e.g., degarelix), anti-androgens (e.g., bicalutamide, enzalutamide), androgen receptor inhibitors (e.g., abiraterone), and combination therapies. Hormone therapy may be administered orally, by injection, or through implantable pellets, depending on the specific medications and treatment regimen.

- ➢ **Duration and Monitoring:** Hormone therapy is typically administered over an extended period, ranging from months to years, depending on the individual patient's response to treatment and disease characteristics. During hormone therapy, patients undergo regular monitoring, including blood tests to assess testosterone levels and imaging studies to evaluate treatment response and disease progression. Adjustments to treatment may be made based on monitoring results and the patient's overall condition.

- ➢ **Side Effects and Management:** Hormone therapy can cause a range of side effects due to testosterone suppression, including hot flashes, decreased libido, erectile dysfunction, fatigue, weight gain, loss of muscle mass, and osteoporosis. Patients may also experience mood changes, depression, and cognitive impairment. Side effects are typically managed with supportive care, medications, and lifestyle modifications to minimize discomfort and improve quality of life.

Chemotherapy

Chemotherapy is a systemic treatment option used in the management of prostate cancer, particularly for patients with advanced or metastatic disease that has spread beyond the prostate gland. Unlike localized treatments such as surgery or radiation therapy, which target specific areas of the body, chemotherapy works by circulating throughout the bloodstream to target and kill rapidly dividing cancer cells wherever they may be in the body.

While not typically used as a first-line treatment for localized prostate cancer, chemotherapy may be recommended in certain cases where the cancer has become resistant to hormone therapy or other treatments, or in combination with other therapies to improve outcomes. Here's an overview of chemotherapy for prostate cancer:

- ➢ **Indications for Chemotherapy:** Chemotherapy may be used in various settings for the treatment of prostate cancer, including as primary therapy for metastatic disease that is not responsive to hormone therapy, in combination with hormone therapy for patients with metastatic hormone-sensitive prostate cancer, or as palliative therapy to relieve symptoms and improve quality of life in patients with advanced or metastatic disease.

- ➢ **Types of Chemotherapy:** There are several chemotherapy drugs used in the treatment of prostate cancer, including docetaxel and cabazitaxel. These drugs work by disrupting the cell division process and inhibiting the growth and proliferation of cancer cells. Chemotherapy drugs may be administered intravenously (IV) in cycles, with periods of treatment followed by rest periods to allow the body to recover from side effects.

- ➢ **Treatment Regimens:** Chemotherapy regimens for prostate cancer may vary depending on factors such as the stage and extent of the disease, the patient's overall health and treatment goals, and the presence of other medical conditions. Treatment plans are typically tailored to each individual patient's needs and may involve a combination of chemotherapy drugs and other therapies such as hormone therapy or targeted therapies.

➢ **Side Effects and Management:** Chemotherapy can cause a range of side effects due to its effects on rapidly dividing cells in the body, including hair follicles, bone marrow, and the gastrointestinal tract. Common side effects of chemotherapy for prostate cancer may include fatigue, nausea and vomiting, loss of appetite, hair loss, mouth sores, diarrhea, and increased risk of infection due to decreased white blood cell counts. Side effects are typically managed with supportive care, medications to alleviate symptoms, and close monitoring for complications.

➢ **Response and Monitoring:** Patients undergoing chemotherapy for prostate cancer are closely monitored throughout treatment to assess treatment response, manage side effects, and adjust treatment as needed. Response to chemotherapy may be evaluated through imaging studies such as CT scans or bone scans, as well as blood tests to monitor tumor markers and overall health status. Adjustments to treatment may be made based on monitoring results and the patient's overall condition.

Immunotherapy

Immunotherapy represents a promising and rapidly evolving treatment approach for prostate cancer, harnessing the body's own immune system to recognize and attack cancer cells. While traditional treatments such as surgery, radiation therapy, and chemotherapy directly target cancer cells, immunotherapy works by stimulating the immune system to recognize and eliminate cancer cells more effectively. Here's an overview of immunotherapy for prostate cancer:

> **Mechanism of Action:** Immunotherapy for prostate cancer works by activating the body's immune response against cancer cells. This can be achieved through various approaches, including immune checkpoint inhibitors, therapeutic vaccines, adoptive

cell therapy, and cytokine therapy. Immune checkpoint inhibitors, such as pembrolizumab and nivolumab, block inhibitory signals that cancer cells use to evade detection by the immune system, allowing immune cells to recognize and attack cancer cells more effectively.

➤ **Indications for Immunotherapy:** Immunotherapy may be used in various settings for the treatment of prostate cancer, including as a primary therapy for metastatic disease that is not responsive to hormone therapy or chemotherapy, in combination with other treatments such as chemotherapy or targeted therapies, or as part of clinical trials investigating novel immunotherapy agents and treatment approaches.

➤ **Types of Immunotherapy:** There are several types of immunotherapy used in the treatment of prostate cancer, each targeting different aspects of the immune system's response to cancer. Therapeutic vaccines, such as sipuleucel-T, stimulate the immune system to recognize and attack prostate cancer cells. Adoptive cell therapy involves infusing patients with immune cells, such as tumor-infiltrating lymphocytes (TILs) or genetically modified T cells, to enhance the immune response against cancer cells. Cytokine therapy involves administering cytokines, such as interleukin-2 or interferon, to boost the activity of immune cells against cancer.

➤ **Treatment Response and Monitoring:** Response to immunotherapy for prostate cancer may vary among patients and depends on factors such as the stage and extent of the disease, the patient's overall health and immune function, and the specific immunotherapy agents used. Response to treatment may be assessed through imaging studies, blood tests, and evaluation of tumor markers to monitor disease progression and treatment effectiveness. Close monitoring is essential for early detection of treatment response or adverse reactions.

➤ **Side Effects and Management:** While immunotherapy offers the potential for durable responses and long-term survival benefits, it can also cause immune-related side effects due to the activation of the immune system. Common side effects of immunotherapy for prostate cancer may include fatigue, rash, diarrhea, nausea, and flu-like symptoms. Immune-related side effects are typically managed with supportive care, medications to suppress immune activity, and close monitoring for complications.

Emerging Treatments and Clinical Trials
Emerging treatments and clinical trials play a pivotal role in advancing the field of prostate cancer treatment, offering new hope for patients by exploring innovative therapies, refining existing treatment approaches, and improving outcomes. These trials investigate promising new drugs, treatment combinations, and therapeutic strategies to address unmet needs and challenges in the management of prostate cancer. Here's an overview of emerging treatments and the importance of clinical trials in prostate cancer:

> **Targeted Therapies:** Targeted therapies represent a promising approach to prostate cancer treatment, focusing on specific molecular targets or pathways involved in cancer growth and progression. These therapies aim to inhibit cancer cell growth

and survival while minimizing damage to normal cells. Targeted therapies for prostate cancer may include drugs that target androgen receptors, such as enzalutamide and abiraterone, as well as inhibitors of other signaling pathways implicated in prostate cancer, such as the PI3K/AKT/mTOR pathway.

➤ **Immunotherapy:** Immunotherapy has emerged as a transformative treatment approach for prostate cancer, harnessing the body's immune system to recognize and attack cancer cells. Immunotherapy agents such as immune checkpoint inhibitors, therapeutic vaccines, and adoptive cell therapies are being investigated in clinical trials for their potential to enhance the immune response against prostate cancer cells and improve treatment outcomes.

➤ **Precision Medicine:** Precision medicine, also known as personalized medicine, aims to tailor treatment strategies to the unique characteristics of individual patients and their tumors. This approach involves identifying specific genetic mutations or molecular alterations driving cancer growth and selecting targeted therapies that are most likely to be effective for each patient. Precision medicine holds great promise for optimizing treatment outcomes and minimizing side effects in prostate cancer patients.

- ➢ **Combination Therapies:** Clinical trials are exploring the potential benefits of combining different treatment modalities, such as surgery, radiation therapy, hormone therapy, chemotherapy, targeted therapies, and immunotherapy, to enhance treatment effectiveness and overcome resistance mechanisms. Combination therapies may target multiple aspects of the cancer biology simultaneously, leading to improved outcomes and prolonged survival for patients with advanced or aggressive prostate cancer.

- ➢ **Importance of Clinical Trials:** Clinical trials are essential for evaluating the safety and efficacy of emerging treatments, advancing scientific knowledge, and improving patient care. Participation in clinical trials provides patients with access to cutting-edge therapies and allows them to contribute to the development of new treatments for prostate cancer. By enrolling in clinical trials, patients can receive innovative treatments that may not be available through standard approaches and help shape the future of prostate cancer treatment for generations to come.

Integrative and Complementary Therapies

Integrative and complementary therapies encompass a diverse range of practices and approaches aimed at enhancing overall well-being, managing symptoms, and improving quality of life for prostate cancer patients.

These therapies, when used in conjunction with conventional medical treatments, can offer a holistic approach to care that addresses the physical, emotional, and spiritual aspects of healing. Here's an overview of integrative and complementary therapies commonly used in the management of prostate cancer:

> **Nutrition and Dietary Supplements:** A healthy diet rich in fruits, vegetables, whole grains, and lean proteins can support overall

health and may help reduce the risk of prostate cancer progression. Some prostate cancer patients also incorporate dietary supplements such as vitamins, minerals, antioxidants, and herbal remedies into their regimen to support immune function, reduce inflammation, and alleviate treatment-related side effects.

> **Exercise and Physical Activity:** Regular exercise and physical activity play a crucial role in maintaining physical fitness, managing stress, and improving overall quality of life for prostate cancer patients. Exercise can help reduce fatigue, improve mood, increase energy levels, and enhance physical function during and after cancer treatment. Activities such as walking, swimming, yoga, tai chi, and strength training can be beneficial for prostate cancer patients of all ages and fitness levels.

> **Mind-Body Therapies:** Mind-body therapies such as meditation, mindfulness, relaxation techniques, guided imagery, and breathing exercises can help reduce stress, anxiety, and depression in prostate cancer patients. These practices promote relaxation,

emotional well-being, and inner peace, enhancing the body's natural healing response and improving overall quality of life.

➢ **Acupuncture and Massage Therapy:** Acupuncture and massage therapy are holistic healing modalities that can help alleviate pain, reduce tension, and promote relaxation in prostate cancer patients. Acupuncture involves the insertion of thin needles into specific points on the body to stimulate energy flow and restore balance, while massage therapy involves manipulating soft tissues to improve circulation, relieve muscle tension, and enhance overall well-being.

➢ **Supportive Care Services:** Supportive care services such as counseling, psychotherapy, support groups, and integrative oncology programs provide emotional support, education, and resources to prostate cancer patients and their families. These services address the psychosocial and spiritual aspects of coping with cancer, helping patients navigate the challenges of diagnosis, treatment, and survivorship with resilience and hope.

CHAPTER 5: DECISION-MAKING PROCESS

Creating a Treatment Team

Creating a comprehensive treatment team is essential for newly diagnosed prostate cancer patients to ensure they receive optimal care, support, and guidance throughout their cancer journey.

A multidisciplinary approach involving healthcare professionals from various specialties allows for a personalized treatment plan tailored to each patient's specific needs and preferences. Here's how to build a treatment team for prostate cancer patients:

> **Urologist or Urologic Oncologist:** A urologist specializing in prostate cancer or a urologic oncologist is often the primary healthcare provider responsible for diagnosing prostate cancer, discussing treatment options, and coordinating care. They perform procedures such as prostate biopsies, surgeries (e.g., prostatectomy), and

provide ongoing monitoring and follow-up care.

➤ **Medical Oncologist:** A medical oncologist specializes in the treatment of cancer using chemotherapy, immunotherapy, targeted therapy, and hormonal therapy. They work closely with patients to develop personalized treatment plans based on the stage and characteristics of the prostate cancer, as well as the patient's overall health and treatment goals.

➤ **Radiation Oncologist:** A radiation oncologist specializes in the use of radiation therapy to treat cancer. They oversee the planning and delivery of radiation treatments, such as external beam radiation therapy or brachytherapy, and monitor patients for treatment response and side effects.

➤ **Nurse Navigator or Patient Advocate:** A nurse navigator or patient advocate serves as a valuable resource and support system for prostate cancer patients, helping them navigate the healthcare system, understand treatment options, coordinate appointments, and access supportive services and resources.

> **Psychosocial Support Team:** Psychosocial support professionals, such as social workers, psychologists, or counselors, provide emotional support, counseling, and resources to help patients cope with the emotional and psychological impact of prostate cancer diagnosis and treatment.

> **Nutritionist or Dietitian:** A nutritionist or dietitian specializes in providing dietary guidance and support to prostate cancer patients, helping them maintain a healthy diet and manage treatment-related side effects such as weight changes, nausea, and fatigue.

> **Physical Therapist:** A physical therapist can assist prostate cancer patients in maintaining physical function, managing treatment-related side effects, and improving quality of life through exercise programs, rehabilitation, and pain management techniques.

Informed Decision-Making

Informed decision-making is a critical aspect of prostate cancer management for newly diagnosed patients, empowering individuals to actively participate in their care, understand their treatment options, and make choices aligned with their values, preferences, and goals. Here's how newly diagnosed prostate cancer patients can engage in informed decision-making:

> **Education and Information:** Patients should seek reliable information and resources about prostate cancer, treatment options, potential side effects, and outcomes from reputable sources such as healthcare providers, patient advocacy organizations, and trusted websites. Understanding the disease and available treatments is the first step toward making informed decisions.

> **Shared Decision-Making:** Shared decision-making involves collaboration between patients and healthcare providers to explore treatment options, discuss risks and benefits, and make decisions that align with the patient's preferences, values, and goals. Patients should actively participate in

discussions with their healthcare team, ask questions, and express their concerns and preferences.

> **Understanding Treatment Options:** Newly diagnosed prostate cancer patients have several treatment options to consider, including surgery (prostatectomy), radiation therapy, hormone therapy, chemotherapy, immunotherapy, and active surveillance. Each treatment option has its own benefits, risks, and potential side effects, which should be thoroughly discussed with healthcare providers to make informed decisions.

> **Consideration of Personal Factors:** Patients should consider their age, overall health, prostate cancer stage and grade, treatment goals, and potential impact on quality of life when making treatment decisions. Factors such as urinary and sexual function, treatment side effects, recovery time, and long-term outcomes should be carefully weighed.

- ➢ **Second Opinions:** Seeking a second opinion from another healthcare provider or specialist can provide additional perspective and information to support decision-making. A second opinion can help confirm a diagnosis, explore alternative treatment options, or provide reassurance about the recommended treatment plan.

- ➢ **Risk Stratification and Prognosis:** Understanding the risk stratification and prognosis of prostate cancer based on factors such as Gleason score, PSA level, and tumor stage can help patients make informed decisions about treatment intensity and aggressiveness.

- ➢ **Emotional Support:** Emotional support from family members, friends, support groups, or mental health professionals can help patients cope with the stress, anxiety, and uncertainty associated with a prostate cancer diagnosis and treatment decision-making process.

Balancing Risks and Benefits

Balancing risks and benefits is a crucial aspect of decision-making for newly diagnosed prostate cancer patients, as they weigh the potential outcomes of various treatment options against their individual preferences, values, and goals.

Each treatment approach carries its own set of risks and benefits, which must be carefully considered to make informed decisions that maximize the likelihood of achieving desired outcomes while minimizing potential harm. Here's how newly diagnosed prostate cancer patients can navigate the process of balancing risks and benefits:

> **Understanding Treatment Options:** Patients should thoroughly explore and understand the risks and benefits of each treatment option available for prostate cancer, including surgery (prostatectomy), radiation therapy, hormone therapy, chemotherapy, immunotherapy, and active surveillance. Healthcare providers can provide detailed information about the potential outcomes, side effects, and long-

term effects of each treatment approach to help patients make informed decisions.

➤ **Assessing Risk Stratification:** Prostate cancer is a heterogeneous disease, ranging from low-risk, indolent tumors to high-risk, aggressive cancers. Patients should undergo risk stratification based on factors such as Gleason score, PSA level, tumor stage, and overall health status to assess the likelihood of disease progression and determine the appropriate level of treatment intensity.

➤ Considering Quality of Life: Treatment decisions should take into account the potential impact on quality of life, including urinary and sexual function, bowel function, physical well-being, emotional well-being, and overall health-related quality of life. Patients should weigh the short-term and long-term effects of treatment against their individual priorities and preferences.

➤ **Consulting with Healthcare Providers:** Patients should engage in open and honest discussions with their healthcare providers about their treatment options, concerns, preferences, and goals. Healthcare providers can provide guidance, support, and expertise to help patients navigate the decision-making process and make choices that are aligned with their values and priorities.

➢ **Seeking Second Opinions:** Seeking a second opinion from another healthcare provider or specialist can provide additional perspective and information to support decision-making. A second opinion can help patients gain clarity, explore alternative treatment options, and make more informed decisions about their care.

➢ **Weighing Short-Term and Long-Term Risks:** Patients should consider both the short-term and long-term risks and benefits of each treatment option when making decisions about prostate cancer management. While some treatments may offer immediate benefits in terms of cancer control, they may also carry long-term risks and side effects that impact quality of life.

CHAPTER 6: SURVIVORSHIP AND FOLLOW-UP CARE

Post-Treatment Monitoring

Post-treatment monitoring is a crucial aspect of prostate cancer management for newly diagnosed patients, ensuring that they receive appropriate follow-up care, surveillance, and support to monitor for disease recurrence, manage treatment-related side effects, and optimize long-term outcomes. Here's an overview of post-treatment monitoring for prostate cancer patients:

> **Follow-Up Visits:** After completing primary treatment for prostate cancer, such as surgery, radiation therapy, or other interventions, patients undergo regular follow-up visits with their healthcare providers to monitor their recovery, assess treatment response, and detect any signs of disease recurrence or progression. Follow-up visits typically occur every few months initially and then less frequently over time, depending on the patient's individual risk profile and treatment history.

- ➢ **PSA Testing:** Prostate-specific antigen (PSA) testing is a standard tool used for monitoring prostate cancer patients after treatment. PSA levels are measured through blood tests to assess the presence of residual cancer cells or recurrence. Rising PSA levels may indicate disease recurrence or progression, prompting further evaluation and intervention.

- ➢ **Digital Rectal Exams (DREs):** Digital rectal exams involve the manual examination of the prostate gland through the rectum to assess for any abnormalities, such as nodules or enlargement, which may suggest recurrence or progression of prostate cancer. DREs are often performed in conjunction with PSA testing to provide a comprehensive assessment of prostate health.

- ➢ **Imaging Studies:** Imaging studies such as MRI, CT scans, bone scans, or PET scans may be performed periodically to evaluate the extent of disease, detect metastases, and monitor treatment response. These imaging modalities provide detailed anatomical and functional information to guide treatment decisions and surveillance strategies.

- ➤ **Monitoring Treatment Side Effects:** Post-treatment monitoring also involves assessing and managing treatment-related side effects, such as urinary incontinence, erectile dysfunction, bowel dysfunction, fatigue, and other issues that may impact quality of life. Healthcare providers work collaboratively with patients to address side effects, provide supportive care, and improve overall well-being.

- ➤ **Psychosocial Support:** Psychosocial support services, including counseling, support groups, and access to resources, are essential for prostate cancer patients to address emotional, psychological, and social concerns related to diagnosis, treatment, and survivorship. These services help patients cope with the challenges of prostate cancer and maintain resilience and well-being throughout their cancer journey.

Survivorship Care Plans

Survivorship care plans are comprehensive documents that provide prostate cancer patients who have completed primary treatment with a roadmap for ongoing care, surveillance, and support to optimize their long-term health and well-being.

These personalized plans are developed in collaboration with healthcare providers and patients to address the unique needs, preferences, and concerns of each individual. Here's an overview of survivorship care plans for newly diagnosed prostate cancer patients:

- ➢ **Treatment Summary:** Survivorship care plans include a detailed summary of the patient's prostate cancer diagnosis, treatment history, and any relevant medical procedures or interventions undergone during the course of treatment. This summary provides a comprehensive overview of the patient's cancer journey and serves as a reference for future healthcare providers.

- ➢ **Follow-Up Care Schedule:** Survivorship care plans outline a recommended schedule for follow-up care and surveillance based on the patient's individual risk profile, treatment history, and specific needs. This schedule typically includes regular visits with healthcare providers, PSA testing, digital rectal exams (DREs), imaging studies, and other assessments to monitor for disease recurrence or progression.

➢ **Monitoring for Treatment Side Effects:** Survivorship care plans address the potential long-term and late effects of prostate cancer treatment, such as urinary incontinence, erectile dysfunction, bowel dysfunction, fatigue, and other issues that may impact quality of life. Patients are provided with guidance on how to recognize, manage, and seek support for treatment-related side effects.

➢ **Health Promotion and Wellness:** Survivorship care plans emphasize the importance of adopting healthy lifestyle behaviors and practices to promote overall health and well-being. Patients receive guidance on nutrition, exercise, stress management, smoking cessation, alcohol moderation, and other lifestyle factors that can positively impact their long-term health outcomes.

- ➢ **Psychosocial Support Services:** Survivorship care plans include information about available psychosocial support services, including counseling, support groups, survivorship programs, and resources to address emotional, psychological, and social concerns related to prostate cancer diagnosis, treatment, and survivorship. These services help patients cope with the challenges of cancer survivorship and maintain resilience and well-being.

- ➢ **Advance Care Planning:** Survivorship care plans may also include discussions about advance care planning, including healthcare directives, end-of-life preferences, and other considerations to ensure that patients' wishes are respected and honored in the event of future healthcare decisions.

Healthy Lifestyle After Treatment

Adopting a healthy lifestyle after prostate cancer treatment is essential for optimizing overall health, reducing the risk of disease recurrence, managing treatment-related side effects, and promoting well-being and quality of life. Here are some key components of a healthy lifestyle for newly diagnosed prostate cancer patients after treatment:

- ➢ **Nutrition:** A well-balanced diet rich in fruits, vegetables, whole grains, lean proteins, and healthy fats is essential for supporting overall health and recovery after prostate cancer treatment. Patients should aim to incorporate a variety of nutrient-dense foods into their diet, limit processed and high-fat foods, and stay hydrated by drinking plenty of water.

- ➢ **Regular Exercise:** Regular physical activity is beneficial for improving physical fitness, managing stress, boosting mood, and reducing the risk of cancer recurrence and other chronic diseases. Prostate cancer survivors should aim to engage in regular exercise, such as walking, swimming, cycling, strength training, or yoga, for at least 30 minutes most days of the week.

➢ **Maintaining a Healthy Weight:** Maintaining a healthy weight through a combination of balanced diet and regular exercise is important for reducing the risk of cancer recurrence and improving overall health and well-being. Patients should aim for a body mass index (BMI) within the healthy range and seek guidance from healthcare providers on weight management strategies if needed.

➢ **Smoking Cessation:** Smoking is associated with an increased risk of cancer recurrence, cardiovascular disease, and other health complications. Prostate cancer survivors who smoke should quit smoking to improve their overall health and reduce the risk of disease recurrence and other adverse outcomes.

➢ **Limiting Alcohol Consumption:** Excessive alcohol consumption is linked to an increased risk of cancer recurrence and other health problems. Prostate cancer survivors should limit their alcohol intake to moderate levels, which is defined as up to one drink per day for men.

> **Stress Management:** Managing stress through relaxation techniques, mindfulness practices, deep breathing exercises, and other stress-reduction strategies can help improve overall well-being and quality of life after prostate cancer treatment. Patients may also benefit from participating in support groups, counseling, or other psychosocial support services to address emotional and psychological concerns.

> **Regular Medical Check-Ups:** Prostate cancer survivors should continue to receive regular medical check-ups, follow-up care, and screenings as recommended by their healthcare providers to monitor for disease recurrence, manage treatment-related side effects, and address any new or ongoing health concerns.

Recurrence and Management

For newly diagnosed prostate cancer patients, the possibility of recurrence is a significant concern, prompting the need for vigilant monitoring and proactive management strategies.

Recurrence occurs when cancer cells return or spread after initial treatment, posing challenges for patients and healthcare providers alike. Here's an overview of recurrence and management strategies for newly diagnosed prostate cancer patients:

> **Understanding Recurrence Risk:** Prostate cancer recurrence can occur locally in the prostate bed, regionally in nearby lymph nodes, or distantly in other parts of the body, such as bones or organs. Recurrence risk depends on factors such as cancer stage, grade, PSA level, treatment history, and individual patient characteristics.

> **Monitoring PSA Levels:** Prostate-specific antigen (PSA) testing is a valuable tool for monitoring disease activity and detecting recurrence after treatment. Rising PSA levels may indicate the presence of residual cancer cells or recurrence, prompting further evaluation and intervention.

> **Digital Rectal Exams (DREs):** Digital rectal exams involve the manual

examination of the prostate gland through the rectum to assess for any abnormalities, such as nodules or enlargement, which may suggest recurrence or progression of prostate cancer.

- ➤ **Imaging Studies:** Imaging studies such as MRI, CT scans, bone scans, or PET scans may be performed to evaluate the extent of disease, detect metastases, and monitor treatment response. These imaging modalities provide detailed anatomical and functional information to guide treatment decisions and surveillance strategies.

- ➤ **Treatment Options for Recurrence:** The management of recurrent prostate cancer depends on various factors, including the location and extent of recurrence, previous treatment history, overall health status, and treatment goals. Treatment options may include salvage radiation therapy, salvage prostatectomy, hormone therapy, chemotherapy, immunotherapy, targeted therapy, or participation in clinical trials investigating novel treatment approaches.

- ➤ **Shared Decision-Making:** Patients should engage in open and honest discussions with their healthcare providers about their treatment options, concerns, preferences, and goals. Shared decision-making involves collaboration between patients and healthcare providers to explore treatment options, discuss risks and benefits, and make decisions that are aligned with the patient's values and priorities.

➢ **Psychosocial Support:** Coping with prostate cancer recurrence can be emotionally challenging for patients and their loved ones. Psychosocial support services, including counseling, support groups, and access to resources, can provide emotional support, guidance, and resources to help patients navigate the challenges of recurrence and maintain resilience and well-being.

CHAPTER 7: 29 DAY MEAL PLAN

Day 1
Breakfast: Avocado Toast
Ingredients:
- Whole grain bread
- Avocado
- Tomato slices
- Olive oil

Instructions: Mash avocado and spread it on toasted whole grain bread. Top with tomato slices and a drizzle of olive oil.

Lunch: Grilled Salmon Salad
Ingredients:
- Grilled salmon
- Mixed greens
- Cherry tomatoes
- Cucumber
- Quinoa
- Lemon vinaigrette dressing

Instructions: Combine grilled salmon, mixed greens, cherry tomatoes, cucumber, and quinoa. Drizzle with lemon vinaigrette.

Dinner: Vegetable Stir-Fry
Ingredients:
- Broccoli
- Bell peppers
- Carrots
- Tofu or lean chicken
- Brown rice
- Low-sodium soy sauce

Instructions: Stir-fry vegetables and tofu or chicken in a pan with low-sodium soy sauce. Serve over brown rice.

Day 2
Breakfast: Greek Yogurt Parfait
Ingredients:
- Greek yogurt
- Berries (blueberries, strawberries)
- Granola
- Honey

Instructions: Layer Greek yogurt with berries and granola. Drizzle with honey.

Lunch: Quinoa and Black Bean Bowl
Ingredients:
- Quinoa
- Black beans
- Corn
- Avocado

> Salsa

Instructions: Mix cooked quinoa with black beans, corn, and diced avocado. Top with salsa.

Dinner: Baked Chicken with Sweet Potato
Ingredients:
- Chicken breast
- Sweet potatoes
- Asparagus
- Olive oil
- Herbs and spices

Instructions: Season chicken and sweet potatoes with herbs and spices. Bake in the oven. Steam asparagus and serve as a side.

Day 3
Breakfast: Oatmeal with Almonds and Berries
Ingredients:
- Rolled oats
- Almond milk
- Almonds
- Berries
- Honey

Instructions: Cook rolled oats with almond milk. Top with almonds, berries, and a drizzle of honey.

Lunch: Lentil Soup
Ingredients:
  - Lentils
  - Carrots
  - Celery
  - Onion
  - Low-sodium vegetable broth

Instructions: Cook lentils with chopped vegetables in low-sodium vegetable broth.

Dinner: Grilled Turkey Burgers
Ingredients:
  - Ground turkey
  - Whole grain buns
  - Lettuce
  - Tomato
  - Onion

Instructions: Form ground turkey into patties and grill. Serve on whole grain buns with lettuce, tomato, and onion.

Day 4
Breakfast: Spinach and Mushroom Omelette
Ingredients:
  - Eggs
  - Spinach
  - Mushrooms
  - Olive oil

➢ Feta cheese (optional)

Instructions: Whisk eggs and pour into a pan with sautéed spinach and mushrooms. Fold in half and cook until eggs are set. Add feta cheese if desired.

Lunch: Chickpea Salad
Ingredients:
- ➢ Chickpeas
- ➢ Cherry tomatoes
- ➢ Cucumber
- ➢ Red onion
- ➢ Feta cheese
- ➢ Olive oil and lemon dressing

Instructions: Combine chickpeas, cherry tomatoes, cucumber, red onion, and feta cheese. Drizzle with olive oil and lemon dressing.

Dinner: Quinoa-Stuffed Peppers
Ingredients:
- ➢ Quinoa
- ➢ Ground turkey or tofu
- ➢ Bell peppers
- ➢ Tomato sauce
- ➢ Italian herbs

Instructions: Cook quinoa and mix with cooked ground turkey or tofu. Cut bell peppers in half, stuff with the mixture, top with tomato sauce, and bake until peppers are tender.

Day 5
Breakfast: Berry Smoothie
Ingredients:
  - Mixed berries (blueberries, raspberries, strawberries)
  - Greek yogurt
  - Almond milk
  - Chia seeds

Instructions: Blend berries, Greek yogurt, almond milk, and chia seeds until smooth.

Lunch: Salmon and Avocado Wrap
Ingredients:
  - Whole grain wrap
  - Grilled salmon
  - Avocado slices
  - Mixed greens
  - Greek yogurt sauce

Instructions: Fill a whole grain wrap with grilled salmon, avocado slices, mixed greens, and a drizzle of Greek yogurt sauce.

Dinner: Vegetable and Lentil Curry
Ingredients:
  - Lentils
  - Mixed vegetables (zucchini, carrots, bell peppers)

➢ Coconut milk
➢ Curry spices

Instructions: Cook lentils and mixed vegetables in coconut milk with curry spices.

Day 6
Breakfast: Whole Grain Pancakes with Berries
Ingredients:
➢ Whole grain pancake mix
➢ Berries
➢ Maple syrup

Instructions: Prepare whole grain pancakes according to package instructions. Top with fresh berries and a drizzle of maple syrup.

Lunch: Turkey and Vegetable Stir-Fry
Ingredients:
➢ Turkey breast strips
➢ Broccoli
➢ Snap peas
➢ Brown rice
➢ Low-sodium teriyaki sauce

Instructions: Stir-fry turkey breast strips and vegetables in a pan with low-sodium teriyaki sauce. Serve over brown rice.

Dinner: Baked Cod with Roasted Vegetables
Ingredients:
- ➤ Cod fillets
- ➤ Sweet potatoes
- ➤ Brussels sprouts
- ➤ Olive oil
- ➤ Lemon

Instructions: Season cod fillets and bake in the oven. Roast sweet potatoes and Brussels sprouts with olive oil and lemon.

Day 7
Breakfast: Chia Seed Pudding
Ingredients:
- ➤ Chia seeds
- ➤ Almond milk
- ➤ Vanilla extract
- ➤ Sliced kiwi and strawberries

Instructions: Mix chia seeds with almond milk and vanilla extract. Refrigerate overnight. Top with sliced kiwi and strawberries.

Lunch: Quinoa Salad with Fruits
Ingredients:
- ➤ Quinoa
- ➤ Mixed greens
- ➤ Mango chunks
- ➤ Pomegranate seeds

- ➢ Walnuts
- ➢ Balsamic vinaigrette

Instructions: Combine cooked quinoa with mixed greens, mango chunks, pomegranate seeds, and walnuts. Drizzle with balsamic vinaigrette.

Dinner: Grilled Vegetable Skewers with Chicken

Ingredients:
- ➢ Chicken breast
- ➢ Bell peppers
- ➢ Zucchini
- ➢ Cherry tomatoes
- ➢ Olive oil and herbs

Instructions: Cut chicken into chunks and thread onto skewers with bell peppers, zucchini, and cherry tomatoes. Grill until chicken is cooked through and vegetables are tender.

Day 8

Breakfast: Whole Grain Toast with Almond Butter and Banana Slices

Ingredients:
- ➢ Whole grain bread
- ➢ Almond butter
- ➢ Banana slices

Instructions: Toast whole grain bread, spread with almond butter, and top with banana slices.

Lunch: Spinach and Berry Salad with Grilled Chicken

Ingredients:
- Grilled chicken breast
- Spinach
- Strawberries
- Blueberries
- Feta cheese
- Balsamic vinaigrette

Instructions: Combine grilled chicken breast with spinach, strawberries, blueberries, and feta cheese. Drizzle with balsamic vinaigrette.

Dinner: Lentil and Vegetable Soup
Ingredients:
- Lentils
- Carrots
- Celery
- Onion
- Low-sodium vegetable broth

Instructions: Cook lentils with chopped vegetables in low-sodium vegetable broth.

Day 9
Breakfast: Smoothie Bowl
Ingredients:
- Greek yogur
- Mixed berries
- Banana slices
- Granola

Instructions: Blend Greek yogurt with mixed berries and pour into a bowl. Top with banana slices and granola.

Lunch: Turkey and Quinoa Stuffed Bell Peppers
Ingredients:
- Ground turkey
- Quinoa
- Bell peppers
- Tomato sauce

> ➤ Italian herbs

Instructions: Cook ground turkey and quinoa. Cut bell peppers in half, stuff with the mixture, top with tomato sauce, and bake until peppers are tender.

Dinner: Grilled Salmon with Lemon-Dill Sauce
Ingredients:
> ➤ Salmon fillets
> ➤ Lemon
> ➤ Fresh dill
> ➤ Olive oil

Instructions: Season salmon fillets with fresh dill and lemon. Grill until the salmon is cooked through.

Day 10
Breakfast: Banana and Walnut Overnight Oats
Ingredients:
> ➤ Rolled oats
> ➤ Almond milk
> ➤ Banana slices
> ➤ Chopped walnuts
> ➤ Maple syrup

Instructions: Mix rolled oats with almond milk, banana slices, chopped walnuts, and a drizzle of maple syrup. Refrigerate overnight.

Lunch: Quinoa and Chickpea Buddha Bowl
Ingredients:
- ➢ Quinoa
- ➢ Chickpeas
- ➢ Roasted sweet potatoes
- ➢ Avocado slices
- ➢ Tahini dressing

Instructions: Arrange cooked quinoa, chickpeas, roasted sweet potatoes, and avocado slices in a bowl. Drizzle with tahini dressing.

Dinner: Baked Chicken Breast with Roasted Vegetables
Ingredients:
- ➢ Chicken breast
- ➢ Brussels sprouts
- ➢ Carrots
- ➢ Olive oil
- ➢ Garlic and herbs

Instructions: Season chicken breast and vegetables with olive oil, garlic, and herbs. Bake until the chicken is cooked through, and the vegetables are tender.

Day 11
Breakfast: Blueberry and Almond Smoothie
Ingredients:
- ➢ Blueberries

➤ Almond milk
➤ Greek yogurt
➤ Almond butter

Instructions: Blend blueberries, almond milk, Greek yogurt, and almond butter until smooth.

Lunch: Spinach and Feta Stuffed Chicken Breast
Ingredients:
➤ Chicken breast
➤ Spinach
➤ Feta cheese
➤ Lemon juice

Instructions: Stuff chicken breast with a mixture of sautéed spinach and feta cheese. Bake until the chicken is cooked through. Drizzle with lemon juice.

Dinner: Vegetable and Lentil Stir-Fry
Ingredients:
➤ Lentils
➤ Broccoli
➤ Bell peppers
➤ Snap peas
➤ Brown rice
➤ Low-sodium soy sauce

Instructions: Stir-fry cooked lentils and vegetables in a pan with low-sodium soy sauce. Serve over brown rice.

Day 12
Breakfast: Whole Grain Waffles with Fresh Berries
Ingredients:
- Whole grain waffle mix
- Mixed berries
- Greek yogurt

Instructions: Prepare whole grain waffles according to the package instructions. Top with mixed berries and a dollop of Greek yogurt.

- Lunch: Shrimp and Quinoa Salad
- Ingredients:
- Shrimp
- Quinoa
- Cherry tomatoes
- Cucumber
- Avocado
- Lemon vinaigrette dressing

Instructions: Cook shrimp and quinoa. Combine with cherry tomatoes, cucumber, and avocado. Drizzle with lemon vinaigrette dressing.

Dinner: Turkey and Vegetable Skewers with Quinoa
Ingredients:

- Ground turkey
- Bell peppers
- Red onion
- Zucchini
- Quinoa

Instructions: Form ground turkey into skewers with bell peppers, red onion, and zucchini. Grill until turkey is cooked. Serve over cooked quinoa.

Day 13
Breakfast: Avocado and Tomato Breakfast Wrap
Ingredients:

- Whole grain wrap
- Avocado slices
- Tomato slices
- Scrambled eggs
- Salsa

Instructions: Fill a whole grain wrap with avocado slices, tomato slices, and scrambled eggs. Top with salsa.

Lunch: Chickpea and Vegetable Curry
Ingredients:

- Chickpeas

- ➢ Mixed vegetables (cauliflower, peas, carrots)
- ➢ Coconut milk
- ➢ Curry spices

Instructions: Cook chickpeas and mixed vegetables in coconut milk with curry spices.

Dinner: Baked Cod with Quinoa and Asparagus

Ingredients:

- ➢ Cod fillets
- ➢ Quinoa
- ➢ Asparagus
- ➢ Lemon
- ➢ Olive oil

Instructions: Season cod fillets and bake in the oven. Serve over cooked quinoa and steamed asparagus. Drizzle with olive oil and lemon.

Day 14

Breakfast: Berry and Spinach Smoothie Bowl

Ingredients:

- ➢ Mixed berries
- ➢ Spinach
- ➢ Banana
- ➢ Almond milk
- ➢ Granola

Instructions: Blend mixed berries, spinach, banana, and almond milk until smooth. Pour into a bowl and top with granola.

Lunch: Turkey and Avocado Wrap
Ingredients:
- Whole grain wrap
- Sliced turkey breast
- Avocado slices
- Lettuce
- Greek yogurt sauce

Instructions: Fill a whole grain wrap with sliced turkey breast, avocado slices, lettuce, and a drizzle of Greek yogurt sauce.

Dinner: Vegetable and Lentil Soup
Ingredients:
- Lentils
- Carrots
- Celery
- Onion
- Low-sodium vegetable broth

Instructions: Cook lentils with chopped vegetables in low-sodium vegetable broth.

Day 15
Breakfast: Overnight Chia Seed Pudding with Mango
Ingredients:
- Chia seeds
- Almond milk
- Mango chunks

➢ Shredded coconut

Instructions: Mix chia seeds with almond milk and mango chunks. Refrigerate overnight. Top with shredded coconut.

Lunch: Quinoa and Black Bean Salad
Ingredients:
➢ Quinoa
➢ Black beans
➢ Corn
➢ Red bell pepper
➢ Cilantro
➢ Lime vinaigrette dressing

Instructions: Combine cooked quinoa with black beans, corn, diced red bell pepper, and cilantro. Drizzle with lime vinaigrette dressing.

Dinner: Grilled Chicken with Roasted Vegetables
Ingredients:
➢ Chicken thighs
➢ Sweet potatoes
➢ Brussels sprouts
➢ Olive oil
➢ Garlic and herbs

Instructions: Season chicken thighs and vegetables with olive oil, garlic, and herbs. Grill chicken and roast vegetables until cooked through.

Day 16
Breakfast: Banana and Almond Butter Smoothie
Ingredients:
- Bananas
- Almond butter
- Greek yogurt
- Almond milk

Instructions: Blend bananas, almond butter, Greek yogurt, and almond milk until smooth.

Lunch: Mediterranean Quinoa Salad
Ingredients:
- Quinoa
- Cherry tomatoes
- Cucumber
- Kalamata olives
- Feta cheese
- Olive oil and lemon dressing

Instructions: Combine cooked quinoa with cherry tomatoes, cucumber, Kalamata olives, and feta cheese. Drizzle with olive oil and lemon dressing.

Dinner: Baked Vegetable Frittata
Ingredients:
- Eggs
- Spinach

- ➤ Bell peppers
- ➤ Onions
- ➤ Tomatoes

Instructions: Whisk eggs and mix with sautéed spinach, bell peppers, onions, and tomatoes. Bake until set.

Day 17

Breakfast: Blueberry and Walnut Oatmeal

- ➤ Ingredients:
- ➤ Rolled oats
- ➤ Almond milk
- ➤ Blueberries
- ➤ Chopped walnuts
- ➤ Maple syrup

Instructions: Cook rolled oats with almond milk. Top with blueberries, chopped walnuts, and a drizzle of maple syrup.

Lunch: Turkey and Vegetable Stir-Fry
Ingredients:

- ➤ Turkey breast
- ➤ Broccoli
- ➤ Snap peas
- ➤ Carrots
- ➤ Brown rice
- ➤ Low-sodium soy sauce

Instructions: Stir-fry turkey breast and vegetables in a pan with low-sodium soy sauce. Serve over brown rice.

Dinner: Grilled Shrimp Skewers with Quinoa

Ingredients:
- Shrimp
- Bell peppers
- Red onion
- Zucchini
- Quinoa

Instructions: Thread shrimp, bell peppers, red onion, and zucchini onto skewers. Grill until shrimp is cooked. Serve over cooked quinoa.

Day 18

Breakfast: Whole Grain Pancakes with Berries

Ingredients:
- Whole grain pancake mix
- Mixed berries
- Greek yogurt

Instructions: Prepare whole grain pancakes according to the package instructions. Top with mixed berries and a dollop of Greek yogurt.

Lunch: Lentil and Vegetable Wrap

Ingredients:
- Lentils
- Spinach

- ➢ Carrots
- ➢ Hummus
- ➢ Whole grain wrap

Instructions: Combine cooked lentils with spinach and carrots. Spread hummus on a whole grain wrap and fill with the lentil mixture.

Dinner: Baked Salmon with Lemon-Dill Sauce
Ingredients:
- ➢ Salmon fillets
- ➢ Lemon
- ➢ Fresh dill
- ➢ Olive oil

Instructions: Season salmon fillets with fresh dill and lemon. Bake in the oven until the salmon is cooked through.

Day 19
Breakfast: Greek Yogurt Parfait
Ingredients:
- ➢ Greek yogurt
- ➢ Granola
- ➢ Mixed berries
- ➢ Honey

Instructions: Layer Greek yogurt with granola and mixed berries. Drizzle with honey.

Lunch: Quinoa and Black Bean Bowl

Ingredients:
- ➢ Quinoa
- ➢ Black beans
- ➢ Corn
- ➢ Avocado
- ➢ Salsa

Instructions: Mix cooked quinoa with black beans, corn, diced avocado, and salsa.

Dinner: Vegetable and Tofu Stir-Fry
Ingredients:
- ➢ Tofu
- ➢ Broccoli
- ➢ Bell peppers
- ➢ Snow peas
- ➢ Brown rice
- ➢ Teriyaki sauce

Instructions: Stir-fry tofu and vegetables in a pan with teriyaki sauce. Serve over brown rice.

Day 20
Breakfast: Spinach and Feta Omelette
Ingredients:
- ➢ Eggs
- ➢ Spinach
- ➢ Feta cheese
- ➢ Cherry tomatoes

Instructions: Whisk eggs and pour into a pan with sautéed spinach, feta cheese, and cherry tomatoes. Fold in half and cook until eggs are set.

Lunch: Chickpea and Vegetable Wrap
Ingredients:
- Chickpeas
- Mixed vegetables (bell peppers, cucumber, lettuce)
- Whole grain wrap
- Tahini dressing

Instructions: Combine chickpeas with mixed vegetables. Fill a whole grain wrap and drizzle with tahini dressing.

Dinner: Grilled Vegetable and Chicken Quinoa Bowl
Ingredients:
- Grilled chicken breast
- Quinoa
- Zucchini
- Bell peppers
- Red onion

Instructions: Grill chicken breast and vegetables. Serve over cooked quinoa.

Day 21
Breakfast: Banana and Berry Smoothie Bowl

Ingredients:
- Bananas
- Mixed berries
- Greek yogurt
- Almond milk
- Granola

Instructions: Blend bananas, mixed berries, Greek yogurt, and almond milk until smooth. Pour into a bowl and top with granola.

Lunch: Turkey and Avocado Salad
Ingredients:
- Sliced turkey breast
- Mixed greens
- Avocado
- Cherry tomatoes
- Balsamic vinaigrette

Instructions: Combine sliced turkey breast with mixed greens, avocado, and cherry tomatoes. Drizzle with balsamic vinaigrette.

Dinner: Baked Cod with Quinoa and Roasted Vegetables
Ingredients:
- Cod fillets
- Quinoa
- Sweet potatoes
- Brussels sprouts

➢ Olive oil

Instructions: Season cod fillets and bake. Serve over cooked quinoa with roasted sweet potatoes and Brussels sprouts. Drizzle with olive oil.

Day 22
Breakfast: Apple Cinnamon Overnight Oats
Ingredients:
➢ Rolled oats
➢ Almond milk
➢ Apple slices
➢ Cinnamon
➢ Maple syrup

Instructions: Mix rolled oats with almond milk, apple slices, cinnamon, and maple syrup. Refrigerate overnight.

Lunch: Spinach and Mushroom Quinoa Bowl
Ingredients:
➢ Quinoa
➢ Spinach
➢ Mushrooms
➢ Cherry tomatoes
➢ Feta cheese

Instructions: Combine cooked quinoa with sautéed spinach, mushrooms, cherry tomatoes, and feta cheese.

Dinner: Grilled Shrimp and Vegetable Skewers with Brown Rice

Ingredients:
- Shrimp
- Bell peppers
- Zucchini
- Brown rice
- Lemon-garlic marinade

Instructions: Thread shrimp and vegetables onto skewers. Grill and serve over brown rice with a lemon-garlic marinade.

Day 23

Breakfast: Whole Grain Toast with Smashed Avocado and Poached Egg

Ingredients:
- Whole grain bread
- Avocado
- Poached egg
- Salt and pepper

Instructions: Toast whole grain bread, spread with smashed avocado, and top with a poached egg. Season with salt and pepper.

Lunch: Lentil and Vegetable Wrap

Ingredients:
- Lentils

> Mixed vegetables (bell peppers, carrots, cucumbers)
> Hummus
> Whole grain wrap

Instructions: Combine cooked lentils with mixed vegetables. Spread hummus on a whole grain wrap and fill with the lentil mixture.

Dinner: Baked Chicken Thighs with Quinoa and Asparagus
Ingredients:
> Chicken thighs
> Quinoa
> Asparagus
> Olive oil
> Herbs and spices

Instructions: Season chicken thighs and bake. Serve over cooked quinoa with roasted asparagus. Drizzle with olive oil and sprinkle with herbs and spices.

Day 24
Breakfast: Mixed Berry and Almond Smoothie
Ingredients:
> Mixed berries
> Almond milk
> Greek yogurt
> Almond butter

Instructions: Blend mixed berries, almond milk, Greek yogurt, and almond butter until smooth.

Lunch: Quinoa and Chickpea Salad
Ingredients:
- Quinoa
- Chickpeas
- Cherry tomatoes
- Cucumber
- Red onion
- Lemon vinaigrette dressing

Instructions: Combine cooked quinoa with chickpeas, cherry tomatoes, cucumber, and red onion. Drizzle with lemon vinaigrette dressing.
- Dinner: Grilled Vegetable and Tofu Stir-Fry
- Ingredients:
- Tofu
- Broccoli
- Bell peppers
- Snow peas
- Brown rice
- Teriyaki sauce

Instructions: Stir-fry tofu and vegetables in a pan with teriyaki sauce. Serve over brown rice.

Day 25
Breakfast: Overnight Chia Seed Pudding with Kiwi
Ingredients:
- Chia seeds
- Almond milk
- Kiwi slices
- Shredded coconut

Instructions: Mix chia seeds with almond milk and kiwi slices. Refrigerate overnight. Top with shredded coconut.

Lunch: Turkey and Vegetable Quinoa Bowl
Ingredients:
- Ground turkey
- Quinoa
- Mixed vegetables (zucchini, bell peppers, carrots)
- Hummus

Instructions: Cook ground turkey and mixed vegetables. Serve over quinoa with a dollop of hummus.

Dinner: Baked Salmon with Lemon-Dill Sauce
Ingredients:
- Salmon fillets
- Lemon
- Fresh dill
- Olive oil

Instructions: Season salmon fillets with fresh dill and lemon. Bake in the oven until cooked through.

Day 26
Breakfast: Greek Yogurt Parfait with Granola
Ingredients:
- Greek yogurt
- Mixed berries
- Granola
- Honey

Instructions: Layer Greek yogurt with mixed berries and granola. Drizzle with honey.

Lunch: Lentil and Vegetable Wrap
Ingredients:
- Lentils
- Spinach
- Tomatoes
- Cucumbers
- Whole grain wrap
- Tahini dressing

Instructions: Combine cooked lentils with spinach, tomatoes, and cucumbers. Fill a whole grain wrap and drizzle with tahini dressing.

Dinner: Grilled Chicken Breast with Quinoa and Roasted Vegetables
Ingredients:
- Chicken breast
- Quinoa
- Bell peppers
- Red onion
- Olive oil

Instructions: Grill chicken breast and vegetables. Serve over cooked quinoa. Drizzle with olive oil.

Day 27
Breakfast: Whole Grain Pancakes with Mixed Berries
Ingredients:
- Whole grain pancake mix
- Mixed berries
- Greek yogurt

Instructions: Prepare whole grain pancakes according to the package instructions. Top with mixed berries and a dollop of Greek yogurt.

Lunch: Chickpea and Vegetable Stir-Fry
Ingredients:
- Chickpeas
- Broccoli
- Snap peas
- Carrots
- Brown rice
- Low-sodium soy sauce

Instructions: Stir-fry chickpeas and vegetables in a pan with low-sodium soy sauce. Serve over brown rice.

Dinner: Baked Cod with Quinoa and Asparagus
Ingredients:
- Cod fillets
- Quinoa
- Asparagus
- Lemon
- Olive oil

Instructions: Season cod fillets and bake. Serve over cooked quinoa with steamed asparagus. Drizzle with olive oil and lemon.

Day 28
Breakfast: Banana and Almond Butter Toast
Ingredients:
- Whole grain bread
- Almond butter
- Banana slices

Instructions: Toast whole grain bread, spread with almond butter, and top with banana slices.

Lunch: Turkey and Avocado Salad
Ingredients:
- Sliced turkey breast
- Mixed greens
- Avocado
- Cherry tomatoes
- Balsamic vinaigrette

Instructions: Combine sliced turkey breast with mixed greens, avocado, and cherry tomatoes. Drizzle with balsamic vinaigrette.

Dinner: Grilled Vegetable and Chicken Quinoa Bowl

Ingredients:

- ➢ Grilled chicken breast
- ➢ Quinoa
- ➢ Zucchini
- ➢ Bell peppers
- ➢ Red onion

Instructions: Grill chicken breast and vegetables. Serve over cooked quinoa.

Day 29
Breakfast: Blueberry and Spinach Smoothie Bowl
Ingredients:
- Blueberries
- Spinach
- Banana
- Almond milk
- Granola

Instructions: Blend blueberries, spinach, banana, and almond milk until smooth. Pour into a bowl and top with granola.

Lunch: Turkey and Vegetable Quinoa Bowl
Ingredients:
- Ground turkey
- Quinoa
- Mixed vegetables (zucchini, bell peppers, carrots)
- Hummus

Instructions: Cook ground turkey and mixed vegetables. Serve over quinoa with a dollop of hummus.

Dinner: Grilled Shrimp and Vegetable Skewers with Brown Rice

Ingredients:

- Shrimp
- Bell peppers
- Zucchini
- Brown rice
- Lemon-garlic marinade

Instructions: Thread shrimp and vegetables onto skewers. Grill and serve over brown rice with a lemon-garlic marinade.

CHAPTER 8: CONCUSSION

Counseling and Therap

Counseling and therapy play a crucial role in supporting the emotional well-being, coping strategies, and overall quality of life for newly diagnosed prostate cancer patients. A prostate cancer diagnosis can evoke a range of emotional responses, including fear, anxiety, sadness, uncertainty, and stress, which may impact patients and their loved ones.

Counseling and therapy provide a safe and supportive space for patients to express their feelings, address concerns, gain coping skills, and navigate the challenges associated with their diagnosis and treatment. Here's how counseling and therapy can benefit newly diagnosed prostate cancer patients:

- ➢ **Emotional Support:** Counseling and therapy offer a valuable opportunity for patients to process their emotions, fears, and concerns related to their prostate cancer diagnosis. Patients may experience a range of emotions, including shock, denial, anger, sadness, and grief, which can be explored and addressed in a non-judgmental and supportive environment.

- ➢ **Coping Strategies:** Counseling and therapy provide patients with coping strategies and skills to manage the emotional and psychological impact of their diagnosis and treatment. Therapists may teach relaxation techniques, mindfulness practices, stress management strategies, and cognitive-behavioral techniques to help patients cope with anxiety, depression, and other emotional challenges.

- ➢ **Communication Skills:** Counseling and therapy can help patients improve their communication skills and enhance their ability to communicate effectively with healthcare providers, family members, and loved ones about their diagnosis, treatment preferences, concerns, and needs. Effective communication can facilitate collaboration, support, and shared decision-making among patients and their support networks.

- ➢ **Supportive Environment:** Counseling and therapy provide a supportive and non-judgmental environment where patients can explore their feelings, beliefs, and concerns without fear of stigma or shame. Therapists offer empathy, validation, and understanding, fostering a sense of connection and validation for patients as they navigate the challenges of their cancer journey.

> **Family and Caregiver Support:** Counseling and therapy extend beyond the individual patient to include family members, partners, and caregivers who may also be impacted by the prostate cancer diagnosis. Family therapy, couples counseling, or support groups can help loved ones navigate their own emotions, roles, and responsibilities, strengthen relationships, and provide mutual support and understanding.

> **Quality of Life:** Counseling and therapy contribute to the overall quality of life for newly diagnosed prostate cancer patients by addressing emotional, psychological, and social concerns that may impact well-being. By providing support, validation, and coping strategies, therapy helps patients navigate the challenges of their diagnosis and

treatment, maintain resilience, and enhance their overall quality of life.

Connecting with Healthcare Professionals

Connecting with healthcare professionals is essential for newly diagnosed prostate cancer patients to receive comprehensive care, support, and guidance throughout their cancer journey.

Building strong relationships with healthcare providers facilitates effective communication, shared decision-making, and personalized treatment planning tailored to each patient's individual needs and preferences. Here's how newly diagnosed prostate cancer patients can connect with healthcare professionals:

- ➢ **Establishing a Healthcare Team:** Newly diagnosed prostate cancer patients should establish a multidisciplinary healthcare team consisting of various specialists, including urologists, medical oncologists, radiation oncologists, nurses, nurse navigators, and other supportive care professionals. This team collaborates to provide comprehensive care and support throughout the cancer journey.

➢ **Open Communication:** Patients should prioritize open and honest communication with their healthcare providers, sharing their concerns, preferences, treatment goals, and questions openly. Effective communication fosters trust, understanding, and collaboration between patients and healthcare providers, leading to better outcomes and patient satisfaction.

➢ **Asking Questions:** Patients should not hesitate to ask questions and seek clarification from their healthcare providers about their prostate cancer diagnosis, treatment options, potential side effects, and prognosis. Asking questions empowers patients to make informed decisions about their care and ensures that they understand their diagnosis and treatment plan fully.

➢ **Seeking Second Opinions:** Seeking a second opinion from another healthcare provider or specialist can provide additional perspective and information to support decision-making. A second opinion can help patients gain clarity, explore alternative treatment options, and make more informed decisions about their care.

- ➢ **Participating in Shared Decision-Making:** Shared decision-making involves collaboration between patients and healthcare providers to explore treatment options, discuss risks and benefits, and make decisions that are aligned with the patient's values and preferences. Patients should actively participate in discussions about their care and advocate for their needs and preferences.

- ➢ **Utilizing Supportive Care Services:** Prostate cancer patients can benefit from accessing supportive care services such as counseling, support groups, survivorship programs, and resources to address emotional, psychological, and social concerns related to their diagnosis and treatment. These services provide valuable support, guidance, and resources to help patients cope with the challenges of cancer and maintain well-being.